DIVAS

Also by Winthrop Sargeant

JAZZ HOT & HYBRID
GENIUSES, GODDESSES AND PEOPLE
LISTENING TO MUSIC
IN SPITE OF MYSELF

Winthrop Sargeant

DIVAS

Coward, McCann & Geoghegan, Inc.
New York

SBN: 698-10489-7
Library of Congress Catalog Card Number: 72-87593

Printed in the United States of America

All but one of the Profiles in this book appeared
originally in *The New Yorker* in slightly different form.

CONTENTS

INTRODUCTION 9

I	JOAN SUTHERLAND	19
II	MARILYN HORNE	48
III	BEVERLY SILLS	74
IV	BIRGIT NILSSON	104
V	LEONTYNE PRICE	134
VI	EILEEN FARRELL	168

Introduction

The word "singer" is used rather loosely nowadays to indicate anyone who can carry a tune and put his vocal cords, no matter how modest their capacities, into action. The microphone has made possible the amplification of even the most minuscule talents, and many a vocalist—many a charming one, it might be added—has made a career singing a pop repertoire over it. Needless to say, this book does not concern that type of artist. It does concern some great singers of the noble art of opera. These singers not only have voices of such power that they can fill an auditorium of approximately four thousand people, such as the Metropolitan Opera House, without amplification and without undue effort, but are also athletes, linguists, musicians, and actors—yes, actors, for despite a legend to the contrary, opera singers can be great actors. To the Broadway public, opera singers seem to conform to a stereotype— overweight, loud, and static. It is true that most of them are robustly built, necessarily so, because big voices seldom reside in slim bodies. The loudness is part of their equipment, but it is always accompanied by a rich, warm quality of tone, and it is not used all the time. The acting of an opera singer who is a great actor is sometimes done with the face and body, as is the case on

Broadway. But more important to the opera buff, it is done with the varied inflections of the voice. Some opera singers are pretty to look at, but that is not their primary appeal in the opera house. The primary appeal is the voice—and the voice of an opera singer is a much more complicated instrument than the nonoperatic public imagines.

Every opera singer has to start with a basic talent—a voice that has a reasonable amount of power or a voice into which power can be built. Generally, vocal experts will tell you that a female singer should not start her vocal studies before adolescence, but it is remarkable how many successful opera singers have started their training shortly after getting out of the cradle. The athleticism of the great opera singer is the fruit of long years of practice. Coloratura technique, in particular (being able to sing trills and run up and down scales hitting every note squarely and in tune), is not a natural endowment. It is cultivated, and many singers continue to work on it throughout their careers. Moreover, opera singers are like baseball players in that their careers are limited to a comparatively short span of their lives, and, again like baseball players, they must make a great deal of money while their gifts are still viable. There are no male singers in this book. That is because today most of the most celebrated names in opera singing are female. There are no Carusos or Björlings among us today. And the female voice has a short period in which it can be heard at its best—usually between the ages of thirty-five and fifty, though some manage a bit longer.

The acquaintance with foreign languages is necessary because all opera, or nearly all (opera in Germany and Italy is an exception), is sung in the language in which it was written. No true opera buff would have it otherwise. The late Giulio Gatti-Casazza, onetime manager of the Metropolitan, once exclaimed, "Opera in English! Heavens no. The public might find out what it's about." And though there is just a grain of truth to this exclamation, especially where the occasional operagoer is concerned, the fact is that the most dedicated of operagoers would feel that his ears were being insulted by, say, a *Carmen* or a *Lucia* in English. There *are* operas that translate perfectly well into English. Those of Mozart and Handel are examples, except perhaps for *Don Giovanni*. But generally the wholehearted romanticism of opera librettos sounds trite or ridiculous when translated. And besides, no true opera lover would want to hear *Faust* or *Pelléas et Mélisande* without the elegant turns of phrase of the original French. The dedicated opera lover is something of a linguist, too. He wants the fluid sound of Italian in his Italian opera and the noble, ponderous sound of German in his German opera. Anyone who doubts the validity of this attitude should listen to *Carmen* sung in German in some German opera house or to Wagner's *Götterdämmerung*, sung in Italy, where its title is usually changed to *Il Crepusculo degli Dei*. The experience is a violation of the intent of the composer and of the sensibilities of the listener.

So opera singers have to be linguists. They don't necessarily have to speak all the languages like a native, though most do. But they do have to have perfect enunciation in several languages, depending on the repertoire they sing, or let's say, they *should* have it. There are a few important singers who pronounce badly; thank God they are in the minority. Most great opera singers, especially those who have reputations as actors, pronounce their lines immaculately. All this is made necessary because opera is very much a European art, the best of it written in Italian, German, and French. But then, so is symphonic music very much a European art. Our musical culture is a transplanted one, and though American composers are hard at work creating a native American style of opera and symphonic music, the bulk of the repertory in both fields is, and will remain for the foreseeable future, European.

In spite of this fact, five of the six singers treated in this book are not Europeans. One is Swedish, one is an Australian, and four are Americans. There is nothing new about American and Australian opera singers. Some of the most famous operatic artists in history—

Geraldine Farrar, Rosa Ponselle, Nellie Melba, Lawrence Tibbett—have been Americans or Australians, and today American opera singers as a group stand very near the top, often outdoing the best Europe has to offer. Where opera in Germany and Austria is generally sung in German, and opera in Italy is sung in Italian, opera in America is sung in its original language. As a consequence, American opera singers are apt to be better linguists than Europeans, except possibly for the English. Today might possibly turn up in history as the golden age of the American opera singer. Americans are singing in nearly every European opera house; they form more than half the roster of the Metropolitan Opera House. In fact, there are not enough opera houses in America to take care of all the able American singers.

Often people who don't particularly like opera are baffled by the enthusiasm and fidelity to the art of those who do like it. And, indeed, there are quite a number of reasons why the dedicated opera lover is crazy about the art. For one thing, it is the most permanent and lasting of theatrical art forms, and it constitutes a sort of museum of past dramatic masterpieces. Goethe, Hugo, Schiller, Scribe, and other great dramatists of the past still live in opera, though their works have pretty much disappeared from the legitimate stage. They were strong dramatists, and their works, embalmed in music, are still capable of causing excitement and reaching the sense of tragedy or comedy. Sophocles and Shakespeare are also prominent in the operatic repertory. Then, of course, there is the music, some of it written by titans like Beethoven and Wagner, some by lesser composers, but always written with great skill in those operas that have remained in the repertory. Of those operas that have not remained in the repertory, some are always being brought to light again. Tens of thousands of operas have been written since the art was first devised in Florence in the sixteenth century. Only a couple of hundred of these are performed year after year.

There is another aspect of opera that has little to do with either the music or the drama, and this is the exploitation of the possibilities of the human voice. The fact is that opera, among other things, is also a sport. The confirmed opera buff is not, as a rule, terribly interested in the visual and purely musical aspects of his two hundredth performance of *Lucia*, though, to be sure, he always enjoys the music and sometimes the drama. What interests him primarily is voices, great voices like those possessed by the subjects of this book. Can Beverly Sills sing as high as Joan Sutherland can? Does this singer possess as clean a coloratura line as that singer? Which has the more powerful voice? What about the difficult register of the middle voice? How does this or that singer cope with it? Who can hit the highest of F's with the most accurate marksmanship? Which one has the finest legato line? I realize that what I am trying to explain makes opera seem a bit like horse racing. And it is. In fact, the sporting aspect of it is what attracts many faithful auditors, especially where Italian opera, and especially Italian opera of the early nineteenth century, is concerned. With German opera and with Verdi and some French opera, things are somewhat different. The music is usually more important than the athletics. But even here, the confirmed operagoer will be interested in judging and comparing singers. They are the lifeblood of the art, and without their competing talents opera would lose half its interest.

There is one other element of the singer's art that is always looked for by the experienced operagoer. This is what is often referred to as style or musicianship. What notes of a phrase are to be accented (sung louder), and what notes are to be allowed to trail off into a soft finish? The artistry of a great operatic artist is often measured by this point. Some artists have a fine style that is instinctive. But most do not. Most have to use their brains in order to achieve fine musicianship, and they also have to counter the natural tendencies of the voice in the process. Some never achieve it. The best example of bad musicianship that I can think of concerns tenors rather than sopranos, and involves the famous aria

13

"Celeste Aida," the aria that appears early in the first act of *Aida*. In fact, "Celeste Aida" is a sort of trap that Verdi has set for bad tenors. All tenors have powerful high notes and love to show them off. A tenor who has a poor style will sing the first phrases of this aria "Celeste Ai*DA*, Forma divi*NA*. The *DA* and the *NA* are high notes lying in the tenor's most powerful range, so he bellows them at full force. Actually, the rhythm of the phrases calls for something else. The stress should fall on the *i* of "Aida" and the *i* of "divina," and the *DA* and *NA* should be left to trail off properly as the endings of the respective phrases. If you have an old Caruso recording of this aria, listen to it. Caruso is too good an artist to murder these phrases, but most of his successors are not that good. Though I can't think of a situation that is comparably simple and graphic in the soprano repertoire, the same thing applies to sopranos. It is a rather subtle point, but no really great singer sings without the kind of musicianship I am referring to.

There are a large number of other, and even subtler, points about opera singing that the dedicated operagoer judges his singers by—the elegant French enunciation that is an absolute must in French opera, the distinction between long and short vowels in Italian, the challenge of projecting fine tone quality in the odd ö's and ü's of French and German, the matter of distinct enunciation in English, when that language turns up, and so on. But since I am not writing a treatise on opera singing, I shall bring this discussion of technical matters to a close.

Sopranos are divided, more or less arbitrarily, into categories. There is the coloratura soprano, who is expected to have enormous agility and the ability to hit high notes accurately. She can be either a dramatic coloratura soprano like Joan Sutherland or a lyric coloratura soprano like Beverly Sills—the difference being in the relative power and weight of the voice. There is the plain lyric soprano or the slightly more agile type that the Italians call *lirico spinto*. Most of Verdi's soprano roles are written for this type of voice, and it is ideally exemplified in Leontyne Price. There is the plain dramatic soprano, a powerful kind of voice, not necessarily very agile, used continually in Wagnerian opera and often in Italian roles too. This is magnificently exemplified by Birgit Nilsson and, with a greater degree of agility, by Eileen Farrell. Then there is the mezzo-soprano, who does not require great agility in Verdi, but who often has it and has to have it for eighteenth- and early-nineteenth-century opera. Marilyn Horne is currently the finest example of this kind of voice. However, she is young by operatic standards, and nobody is quite sure what kind of soprano she will eventually develop into. I hasten to add that these classifications are mere approximations. There are singers who overlap from one to the other. There are singers who are so specialized that they occupy only a small area of each, and there are singers who can manage two or three of the categories at the same time.

Finally, I would like to stress a few things about the personality of sopranos. They are all healthy specimens, for good health is one of the basic requirements of a singer. On the other hand, the human voice is a very delicate instrument, and anything in the way of a cold or other respiratory problem can temporarily ruin it. Sopranos have good and bad days. The monthly problems of the female physique can disturb a voice greatly. So all sopranos do not always sing exactly as well at every performance. Though one or two of the singers in this book suffer from severe personal problems in their offstage life, sopranos, in fact, all singers, are apt to be happy people and are apt to project a feeling of happiness to their audiences. Singing is the healthiest of the performing arts. More air, sometimes fresh, sometimes not, is inhaled and exhaled by them than by anybody else in the performing field. Most of them love to eat, and a great many of them run to fat as their careers progress, but this usually enhances their vocal qualities, which are the main interest of operagoers. I have, in the coming chapters, analyzed the personalities and careers of six sopranos who might be called superstars, that term meaning only that they make a great deal of money (up to ten thousand dollars) for each appearance, though they don't make quite that much at the Metropolitan

Opera House, and the one who sings with the New York City Opera (Beverly Sills) appears there for very little in the way of remuneration. Generally recitals are more remunerative than operatic appearances. But, in a way, all this is irrelevant. Most singers would sing whether they were paid for it or not.

There is another factor in today's singing that is unique to its period and that is worth considering. Operagoers, especially elderly ones, are always talking about the "good old days" or the "golden era" when singers sang much better than they do today. This is an illusion. As I mentioned above, some of the last singers of the "golden age" whom we can listen to on old recordings turn out to have been pretty sloppy as artists. But there is also another point that has to do with this problem. Henry Pleasants, a distinguished American critic active in London, once put it in a nutshell in an article entitled "How High Was G?" in the February 20, 1971, *Opera News*. The point is that, over the past hundred years the pitch (difference between high and low) of what one hears has gone up and up. This is mainly because orchestras sound more brilliant if their instruments are tuned up higher than was expected by nineteenth-century composers, and they have tended to be tuned higher and higher with each generation. The current standard of pitch demands that the A above middle C be tuned to 440 vibrations per second, or somewhere in that neighborhood. And, as a concert progresses, both stringed instruments and wind instruments become warmer, and their pitch rises in consequence, sometimes reaching as much as 445 vibrations per second. Now, in Beethoven's day, prevailing pitches hovered around 435 vibrations per second, and all orchestras played with their instruments tuned at that much lower figure. The difference between 435 and 445 vibrations per second can be more than a half tone and perhaps an even larger interval. The human voice is not tuned like an instrument. There is a limit to its reach in the direction of high notes. A singer who is singing Beethoven's *Fidelio*, for example, today sings it between a half and a whole tone higher than a singer did in Beethoven's day, and the pitch conventions of Beethoven's day were used by opera composers like Rossini, Bellini, and Donizetti. A soprano singing *Lucia* has high C's, D's and E's written for her according to the pitch of Donizetti's period, but she is singing them according to the demands of present-day orchestras. This means that a high C has actually become a high D, or something in its neighborhood, and a high F (which is ordinarily the highest note demanded of a coloratura soprano) is nowadays approximately a high G, a note that singers of Pasta's and Malibran's day were not expected to be able to sing. Today it is sung; and brilliantly too. Many people are worried about the extra strain that this change involves for the opera singer. But there is not a ghost of a chance that orchestras will agree to tune themselves down to the pitch of Beethoven's period. That course would make singing much easier, but it would also make orchestras sound dull and damp. Occasionally a singer will demand transpositions downward in order to counter this tendency—they will ask, for example, that an aria written in the key of C be played by the orchestra in the key of B-flat, and the orchestra parts in most opera houses are prepared for such transpositions, with little bridge passages that make them sound natural. But the greatest singers do not demand transposition. They accept the challenge of the higher pitch and bring off their arias with ease in spite of it. This is one reason to believe that today's singers belong to a golden age of their own and are, in many ways, superior to the singers of the past—superior not only in musicianship and vocal technique, but in the spread of their range as well. None of the singers mentioned in this book demands transposition. They accept the challenge, and manage magnificently, singing everything at a much higher pitch than their famous nineteenth-century forebears. I think that this feat deserves a special accolade. Today's great sopranos are better singers than any of the famous names that you find in history books or musical dictionaries. The "golden age," where sopranos are concerned, is now.

Miss Sutherland as Norma in Bellini's *Norma*—with the Vancouver Opera Association.

I
Joan Sutherland

Photograph by Tony Rollo (Newsweek)

Joan Sutherland and her son, Adam, in her dressing room after she had made her debut at the Metropolitan Opera House in 1961.

On February 21, 1961, a tall, red-haired, square-jawed soprano made her New York debut at Town Hall in a concert performance of Bellini's *Beatrice di Tenda*. It was a production of the American Opera Society, at whose concerts most of music's operatic intelligentsia were to be found. She was an Australian named Joan Sutherland. She had been preceded by glowing reports from London and by a recording of Handel's *Acis and Galatea* on which record buffs had detected a voice of remarkable agility. She had previously appeared in Vancouver and Dallas, where critics had unearthed special adjectives to describe her singing. But, after all, this was New York, and her successes had all been out of town. The debut was a modest one. Town Hall is a small auditorium. But her success was so phenomenal that two more performances were held, in Carnegie Hall, in response to public demand. Critics forgot about all the other singers in the cast. Miss Sutherland unquestionably had the most remarkable voice they had heard in at least a couple of generations. It was as large as that of a topranking Wagnerian soprano. It had a range that stretched from A below middle C to F, or even to F-sharp, above the staff. It also had the sensuous, womanly quality that proclaims the great diva. But the

21

most glorious things about it were its astonishing agility and its uncanny accuracy. The agility, which enabled her to toss off scales, arpeggios, and trills, was familiar enough in connection with small voices but almost unprecedented in voices of Miss Sutherland's power. The accuracy with which she could sing every note of a rapid scale in perfect tune, or hit a high F squarely and with consummate ease and full power, was something that sent voice buffs to their history books, where comparable feats were recorded only by Giuditta Pasta and Maria Malibran, during the first half of the nineteenth century. Miss Sutherland seemed to use only a part of her lung power, leaving plenty of reserve breath in case of need—the mark of absolute vocal mastery. Her musicianship (what musicians call style—the knowledge of where to place accents and where to let the voice trail off) was immaculate. Most impressive of all, perhaps, was the complete assurance with which she attacked her florid arias. Nobody in her audience worried about whether she would hit those lofty bull's-eyes that were written expressly to exhibit the marksmanship of sopranos of her type—high C's, D's, E's, and F's. Where the average coloratura soprano squeaked, Miss Sutherland sang, and sang magnificently. The following November, the Metropolitan Opera presented her in Donizetti's *Lucia di Lammermoor,* in which she sang the role of Sir Walter Scott's heroine with extraordinary power, and acted it with an earnest realism that held her audience spellbound. It was not long before Miss Sutherland was being called "the greatest singer of the century" and "the living glory of the operatic stage." Even the most learned critics could not recall an experience or trace a record that gave any grounds for denying these assertions.

In a way, Miss Sutherland was the culmination of a revival that had been initiated a decade or so earlier by the famous soprano Maria Callas, along with the Italian conductors Vittorio Gui and Tullio Serafin. This revival entailed the resuscitation of an operatic style, and thus of a great many operas, that had fallen into neglect simply for lack of singers who could sing them adequately. The style is known as bel canto, which in Italian means simply "beautiful singing," and the resuscitated operas dated from the eighteenth and early nineteenth centuries, when sheer vocalism rather than dramatic realism was required. The most famous composers of bel-canto operas were George Frederick Handel (1685-1759); Gioacchino Rossini (1792-1868), whose *Barber of Seville* had survived in the standard repertory partly because of its farcical plot, partly because of its delightful score; Gaetano Donizetti (1797-1848); and Vincenzo Bellini (1801-35). For these composers, the exhibition of vocal athletics was the main purpose of their writing. They happily sent their female characters to the execution block or drove them mad in order to allow them the most ebullient and splashy concatenations of vocal fireworks. And people went to these operas purely for the joy of hearing magnificent voices engage in incredible vocal feats. Later on, bel canto fell out of fashion. Among other things, it was felt to be too artificial, too unrelated to reality. Composers like Verdi made opera into a more or less realistic kind of theater, and demanded more emotional involvement and more acting ability from their singers while lessening their purely athletic duties. Richard Wagner, Verdi's great German rival, subordinated the singers to the orchestra, and gave them roles that required power of voice and an ability to project emotion. Still later, the Italian school of *verismo*, under Leoncavallo, Mascagni, and Puccini, sought the ultimate in realism by having singers act out modern, or fairly modern, stories, and burst into real song only at climactic moments—and quite elementary song at that. The fashions of opera had reached the opposite pole—drama, rather than singing pure and simple—and the works of the bel-canto period were, with few exceptions, discarded and forgotten.

Then, as the level of vocal writing continued to decline under the *verismo* school, singers and musicians began poking into the archives of the past, and rediscovered bel-canto opera. The difficulty was to find singers capable of undertaking this old repertory. The operas were melodious and musically engaging, but they demanded a type of singer that seemed to have become extinct. The great Maria Callas finally came along to fill the requirements. She could sing all the brilliant fioritura flawlessly, and, pressed on by the conductors Gui and Serafin, she managed to make the bel-canto operas exciting again. People once more began attending operas purely to hear brilliant athletic singing, and Handel, Rossini, Donizetti, and Bellini suddenly reemerged as opera composers. Unfortunately, Miss Callas, a striking actress as well as a superb singer, undertook roles that were more and more difficult, and, being a rather plump woman (as most great sopranos are), she decided to diet until she had a beautiful figure. She got the beautiful figure, but in the process she severely damaged her voice. She had racked up a decade and a half of stunning performances, and nobody who heard her during this period will ever forget them. She had also set the revival of bel-canto singing on its way, pioneering the territory that Miss Sutherland was to inherit. By the time people were calling Miss Sutherland the greatest singer of the century, Miss Callas was singing less and less, but the vogue for bel canto was still raging, and Miss Sutherland became its most adulated figure.

There was plenty of reason for the adulation. There was the infinitely supple and infinitely powerful Sutherland voice—a product not only of natural endowment, but of years of patient training. There was also the flawless musicianship, and this brings us to another feature of the Sutherland phenomenon—a quiet, dark-eyed man named Richard Bonynge (pronounced "Bonning"), who is almost as responsible for Miss Sutherland's eminence as she herself is. Ricky Bonynge has been Miss Sutherland's close collaborator since they were both teen-agers in Australia, and he has been for some time her husband as well as her principal coach.

(Every important opera singer has two indispensable helpers—his vocal teacher, who has taught him how to use his voice, and his coach, who goes over all his roles with him, patiently explaining matters of diction, musical style, and dramatic inflection while pounding the role into his memory at the piano.) Mr. Bonynge is a dark, handsome, saturnine-looking man whose saturninity melts into effusive gentleness after a few minutes of acquaintance. He is a great scholar of bel-canto opera, the discoverer of original bel-canto manuscripts in out-of-the way places, an expert in the art of ornamentation—those turns and arpeggios that a bel-canto singer is supposed to improvise—and a pianist of considerable attainments. He is not exactly a Svengali; Miss Sutherland herself knows every trick of vocal production and how to use her remarkable voice. But, like all prominent singers, she needs a coach to smooth out her interpretations, correct her pronunciation of foreign languages, and act as a continuous critic of what she does. (No singer ever hears himself as others hear him. He needs an outside reaction to make sure that what is going on in his lungs, throat, and head is coming out as he wishes it to.) Yet Bonynge is not merely Joan Sutherland's coach and husband. He is—as she freely and enthusiastically concedes—largely responsible for her present career. It was he who, two decades ago, insisted that she could be the world's greatest coloratura soprano instead of the Wagnerian singer she then contemplated being. It was he who gradually lifted the range of her voice—sometimes by deception. He used to transpose his accompaniments to her vocalises, or voice exercises, higher and higher, and Miss Sutherland, who does not have perfect pitch, did not realize what was being done until she suddenly found herself singing high E's and F's. It was he who bullied and cajoled her into attempting coloratura roles that she would never have undertaken by herself. Miss Sutherland left to her own devices would still have been an important singer. But without Bonynge's continuous prodding she never would have been the singer she is

25

today. "I think I have a lazy temperament," she said recently. "Basically, I'm a very timid person. Don't think that Ricky's pushy, but he's certainly a driving force. And a great sort of ego booster, really. He may tear me down from having any illusions about how good I might be, but if I do something really extraordinary, he's the first one to say so. He's always had incredible faith in my having the sort of career I've had." Mr. Bonynge has devoted almost his entire life to Miss Sutherland's voice, and nowadays he almost always presides as conductor in the orchestra pit when she sings.

Unlike most opera singers, Miss Sutherland is not a natural extrovert. She is a shy woman who is easily embarrassed, and she cares very little about the glamorous aspects of being a great diva. After-the-opera parties do not interest her; she usually goes straight home following the last curtain call. Home, in New York, is two floors of an elegant old mansion overlooking Prospect Park, in Brooklyn, owned by Martin Waldron, a voice and speech teacher at the Neighborhood Playhouse School of the Theatre, who is a great admirer of her voice; he insists that the Bonynges use his two top floors during the two or three months a year they spend here. (The Bonynges used to live on West Ninth Street, in Greenwich Village, but when that bomb demolished the house on West Eleventh Street—they heard the explosion—they decided to move to a less anarchic part of town.) The two floors, furnished by the Bonynges, are rather somber and satisfyingly old-fashioned, with gloomy pictures on the walls and a huge collection of posters and photographs recalling the time of Pavlova. (Mr. Bonynge has recorded the ballets she danced in.) The Bonynges do not like to stay in hotels. "I find them very impersonal," Miss Sutherland said the other day. "You aren't able to relax much. You either have to go out for meals or have them sent up by room service. I hate to eat before a rehearsal or before a performance, and it isn't always easy to get meals at odd hours. We live a very irregular schedule.

You don't feel that you want to work after a nice dinner—you just want to sit around and chat. We have a good lunch around half past one or quarter to two, and then we have a light meal—maybe scrambled eggs and a salad—after the performance. I never eat anything *before* a performance." Once at home, Miss Sutherland becomes very domestic. Indeed, many Brooklynites have seen a large redheaded woman pass by, pushing a shopping cart, without having the slightest idea who she is. Being on the international operatic circuit, the Bonynges actually have several homes—a flat in London and a chalet above the Lake of Geneva, in Switzerland, which they consider their permanent residence, though they seldom get a chance to spend more than two and a half months a year there, in summer, and even then the recording companies are always trying to lure them away. There they commune briefly with their only child, Adam, who is otherwise taken care of by a Swiss housekeeper named Ruthli. They do a good deal of worrying about Adam, wondering whether he feels unloved or otherwise neglected. They have noticed that when they go to Switzerland, Adam, as often as not, goes off somewhere else with his pals.

Miss Sutherland is a big woman, standing five feet eight and a half in her stockings and weighing anywhere between a hundred and seventy and somewhat over two hundred pounds. When she is not thinking carefully about her English pronunciation, she lapses into a slight but detectable Australian accent. Like all successful opera singers, she is a fairly robust specimen, and she wouldn't for the world think of dieting, because she is sure it would damage her voice. Beneath the crown of red hair, a pair of hazel eyes, and a small nose and a large mouth is that square, Scottish jaw that keeps her from being a conventional beauty. Miss Sutherland has always been conscious of a certain awkwardness in her physical appearance. "I know I'm not exactly a bombshell," she said recently, "but one has to make the best of what one's got." And making the best in her case involves, among other things, a strong sensitiveness

27

toward and a great consideration for others. She is widely known as "the great lady of opera." She has never been heard to criticize or put down a rival singer. Offstage, she is unassuming, natural, and nearly always composed. She has evolved a personal philosophy that resolves itself into the motto "Simplicity, serenity, sincerity." There are, of course, certain stresses and strains connected with her professional life, and once or twice she has had a real row—usually with a conductor whom she considered pigheaded. But she is inclined to deplore such incidents and to regret that the press has taken note of them. "I think I have a reasonably placid temperament," she has said. "If I weren't reasonably placid, I don't think I could cope with this sort of life. To be a diva, you've got to be absolutely like a horse. Sometimes I get upset, and then I upset other people. I don't like to do that. That's when I get mad at myself. Mostly when I get mad, it's at myself."

As opera singers go, Miss Sutherland is a slow learner, and she has a very bad memory. Once, in Chicago, she sang the baritone's cadenza by mistake instead of her own. On another occasion there, she got lost in a cadenza and improvised for a full minute, finally getting back to the proper place, while Bonynge and her more knowing auditors held their breath. Many people have noticed that at recitals Miss Sutherland always has a book or a sheet of music in her hand. At a concert at the Kennedy Center, in Washington, a woman interrupted the proceedings by rising from her seat between numbers and asking loudly, "Why do you have to have that book in your hand?" The rest of the audience waited in silence, as if stunned. It was an awkward moment. But Miss Sutherland took it in her stride. She replied calmly, "I have no memory. Either I have a book or I don't sing." Her placidity and her warmth have been credited with calming and humanizing other singers with whom she has worked. The famous American mezzo-soprano Marilyn Horne regards her with awe, and so does the even more famous

Renata Tebaldi. Miss Sutherland has taught Miss Horne to do needlepoint, a skill with which she herself occupies most of her spare time, and one that promotes serenity of mind. Her husband maintains that she once did a whole needlepoint rug, but she claims that it was only a small mat. In any event, the needlepoint goes on month after month and year after year, and there is scarcely a friend who has not at one time or another been presented with a needlepoint cushion cover or table mat. Miss Sutherland has a strong character. She works constantly either at needlepoint or at her singing roles, and almost never indulges in any sort of frivolity.

The strong character is essential, for in pursuing her career she has had to overcome handicaps that might have overwhelmed any other singer. Despite her generally stalwart physique, Miss Sutherland has been a continual victim of minor ailments, which in her case have assumed major proportions. Though her vocal cords have been pronounced the most nearly perfect imaginable by doctors, the area above them—throat, sinus passages, and mouth—has been a source of incessant trouble and agony. She is plagued by abscesses of the ear, and has undergone painful operations to clear her sinuses. She has often sung brilliant performances while partly deaf. At the start of her career, she had bad trouble with her teeth, and after years of dental difficulties they had to be capped. In addition to all this, she has suffered for years, and still suffers, from acute back trouble. She underwent treatment by acupuncture in London some years ago, and claimed that it worked—temporarily—but her back still goes out from time to time, and since 1960 she has worn a surgical corset. She has crippling back spasms that require the ministrations of a masseuse, and so frequent have these spasms become that she has located a specialist in every city where she is likely to sing. (In New York she has massages at least twice a week.) She also has poor circulation in her lower extremities, and has now and then sung performances with swollen legs bandaged from ankle to knee. Few in her audiences have ever realized what. an effort of will is involved in singing a work like *Norma,* in which she is onstage during practically the entire evening.

Such exertions do a lot to explain her behavior after performances. In Chicago, a great banquet was held following her appearance in Rossini's *Semiramide.* Trumpets played a fanfare as she entered the dining hall. But Miss Sutherland, after a few smiles and bows, simply said, "I'm tired—I want to go home," and departed forthwith. Actually, her back trouble is so severe that although she can stand or lie down, she cannot sit for any length of time, and this, in an age of jet travel for divas, is a serious matter. It probably explains why she remains for several months in one place, instead of flying back and forth all over the world, as some divas do.

Russell Braddon, who has written a biography of Miss Sutherland, has speculated about whether or not she sings better when she is angry (some singers do), and he recollects an incident when she was singing Desdemona to Ramón Vinay's Otello in London—actually, the performance that gave her her first push toward stardom. According to Mr. Braddon, Mr. Vinay laid hold of Miss Sutherland and hurled her across the floor and into a pillar, after which, furious, she sang like an angel. Miss Sutherland doesn't seem to remember the occasion that way, but she doesn't 'deny that it could have happened. "Some people do have the idea that if I get mad I sing much better," she said. "I don't know whether it's true or not. It's a theory, but I hate to believe it, because I hate to think that one can get mad in this kind of profession. I get mad at myself if a performance doesn't go the way I want it to. But it's no use getting mad at other people. They haven't got much to do with it, you know. I sometimes lose my temper—don't we all? I think one loses one's temper easily if one is tired." At a performance of *La Sonnambula* in the Fenice opera house in Venice some years ago, she was not only tired, but thoroughly banged up from a slip in a bathtub. "There was one of those little squabbles that shouldn't get into the papers," she said. "It was a question of tempos. I wanted the tempo of Maestro Serafin, with whom I had sung the part. The Fenice conductor wanted it different. I still maintain that he was wrong. He was very rude to me—he said, 'Madame, I am the conductor here'—and he was very rude to the chorus master also. A bad patch." Miss Sutherland walked out after this occurrence and has never sung with that conductor again. She was insisting on a prerogative dating from the bel-canto period—that a singer must set his own tempos according to his breathing capacity and his current feeling about his agility in fioritura, and that it is the conductor's duty to follow.

Miss Sutherland has had other rows with conductors. One of them, at Covent Garden, was with Rafael Kubelik (now the musical director at the Met), who wanted her to speak Micaela's dialogue before her third-act aria in *Carmen*. Miss Sutherland objected strenuously to the spoken dialogue, which has not been traditional since the recitatives were written, shortly after Bizet's death. Moreover, she explains, the opera was being done in English, and the number of differing accents at Covent Garden— Australian, Welsh, Irish, German—made spoken dialogue ridiculous. She won the argument that time. "I think Mr. Kubelik is going to throw me out of the Metropolitan," she said jokingly. "Of course, I have seen him since, and I may be wrong. I seem to recollect that I did *Die Meistersinger* with him after that." Still another contretemps erupted with Vittorio Gui at La Scala. Maestro Gui had concocted an ending of his own for Bellini's *Beatrice di Tenda* because he considered Bellini's ending too flamboyant. The Bonynges felt that Miss Sutherland should sing exactly what Bellini had written. Maestro Gui had strenuous objections. He wanted his own ending. Miss Sutherland refused to do it, and Maestro Gui, too, was adamant. La Scala eventually had to find another conductor to take his place.

Miss Sutherland's favorite conductor is her husband. Mr. Bonynge has from time to time been severely criticized for vacillating tempos and weak rhythms, but from a singer's point of view—and especially from the point of view of a bel-canto singer—he is the ideal maestro. He never pushes the vocalist with insistent rhythms. He follows the vocal line, allowing the singer to set his own pace, which may differ from one performance to another, depending on the agility of the moment or the supply of breath. He is acutely conscious of breathing problems, and he tailors his orchestral accompaniment to suit. And Miss Sutherland is not by any means the only singer who likes to sing with him. Martina Arroyo, Marilyn Horne, Huguette Tourangeau, Spiro Malas, and others have expressed gratification at the way he handles the accompaniments to their arias. "I have never known a singer who didn't love him after the performance," Terry McEwen, an old friend of the Bonynges', who is now the manager of the classical division of London Records here, once remarked. Mr. Bonynge's method would not work with operas of the late nineteenth or early twentieth century. But for bel-canto opera, where the voice is the thing, he has special endowments. Most of them arise from a lifelong devotion to voices and from a modest conception of his role as conductor. Very early in his life, he became more interested in voices than in his own métier as a pianist. He has frequently discovered vocal talent, has given unsparingly of his time to coach singers, and is happiest when he is thumping out a bel-canto accompaniment while steering a voice this way or that. Miss Sutherland maintains that he has a sort of ESP where singers are concerned. His abilities as a coach are apparently phenomenal, and none of the singers on the stage while he is conducting are in danger of losing their composure. He props them up at every juncture.

The only thing Miss Sutherland has ever been criticized for is her indistinct and sometimes distorted enunciation of the words she sings. Her diction is often poor. Taxed with this by an interviewer, she replied, "To me, I'm singing the words perfectly—as clear as a little bell." Then, on reflection, she added, "It's possible that I lose the awareness of them." But the fact remains that she is apt to begin the famous aria "Casta diva" "Coosta diva." Mr. McEwen has his own explanation of this. He thinks that Miss Sutherland, being a very canny singer, is in the habit of "covering" her vowel sounds so that they do not strain her voice. "Joan will still be singing twenty years from now," he says. "Her voice will never wear out, because she takes such good care of it. And her peculiar diction is part of this care. She used to sing brighter than she does now. But she's learned to conserve her voice. Also, she seldom goes overboard onstage. She is never overinvolved. This, too, protects her voice."

In any case, though critics may complain, Miss Sutherland is not likely to change her habits in this matter. She does not bother to warm up before a performance, as most singers do, and she quotes the great tenor Jussi Bjorling on the subject: "If you feel well, it isn't necessary; if you don't feel well, it doesn't do any good." Her attitude toward critics is independently Australian. "I think anyone is flattered if somebody likes one, don't you?" she says. "But I think Australians have a sort of independence, and I think that, rightly or wrongly, they tend to make their own decisions as to how a thing has gone. Pioneers are apt to be like that. I think that it's not a bad idea. You can listen to what everybody says, but the fact remains that you've got to get out there and do the thing yourself."

At home with her husband in their somber, old-fashioned Brooklyn apartment, Miss Sutherland does a good deal of reading, besides her interminable needlepoint. She likes history books and historical novels about early England. (She is particularly fascinated by King Arthur and Merlin.) "I read a lot of lighter stuff, too, like Helen MacInnes, and I like suspense stories," she said recently. "I'm tired of Agatha Christie, though. She's too predictable. I also write a lot of letters. I have so many friends all around the world." Actually, though, the Bonynges are not particularly sociable. A few intimate friends constitute their circle. Their countless admirers are outsiders as far as their private life is concerned. And most of Miss Sutherland's correspondents are old acquaintances from Australia and the London days.

Australia—or, to be more exact, the southeastern part of Australia, which is where Miss Sutherland comes from—has a curious relation to the art of singing. It has produced a remarkable number of singers, considering its sparse population. Nellie Melba, the operatic paragon of the 1890's, was born near Melbourne. Florence Austral, an important Wagnerian soprano of a slightly later time, was born in Melbourne. The great Wagnerian soprano Marjorie Lawrence was born in the vicinity. And the late John Brownlee, a noble baritone who shone especially in French opera, was born in the seaport town of Geelong, fifty miles from Melbourne. As for Miss Sutherland, she was born in Sydney, of almost pure Scottish parentage, about forty years ago. Her father, William Sutherland, born in Scotland, was a master tailor, and her mother, Muriel, whose family had come to Australia earlier, had a Scottish father. William Sutherland's family was a large one. In addition to Joan and her sister, Barbara, there were four children by a former wife. By the time Joan was born, the Depression had hit Australia, and the family was in straitened circumstances, with debts piling up and no great demand for tailored suits. Her father died when she was six, leaving the family even worse off. They moved to their grandfather's house, and her mother as well as her older half sisters went to work. Two things, even at the early time, pointed to a singing career. Joan's mother had a fine contralto voice, and Joan, from the age of three, sat beside her at the piano while she did her vocalises, often joining in herself. Her mother had never contemplated a vocal career. "Heavens, no," Miss

Sutherland said the other day. "Mother would rather have gone to the races." The other early influence was Cousin John, a very prosperous tanner and real-estate man. "Australians are great collectors of recordings," Miss Sutherland said. "They are so far away from the big centers of opera." And Cousin John had a big collection of records by people like Galli-Curci and Caruso. Listening to them, Joan began to imitate Galli-Curci. Then she was hired to sing on a children's radio show, but her mother came to disapprove of it (Joan was only seven) and kept her at home, seeing to it that she had piano lessons. When Joan was eight, she was sent to St. Catherine's Church of England School for Girls, which happened to be nearby. (The family was strict Presbyterian, and attended church regularly.) She was a big girl from the beginning; she wanted to play the part of a fairy in the school play, but they cast her as a giant instead. When she was twelve, her mother took her to her first concert, in the Sydney Town Hall, and she confessed that she wanted to sing there someday. But she was not yet confident of her ability. So after graduation from school, at fifteen, she took a secretarial course and became a typist in an office. At about this time, she read an advertisement in the Sydney *Morning Herald* in which a two-year singing scholarship was offered by a couple of voice teachers named John and Aida Dickens. She auditioned and won the scholarship. John Dickens was a tyrannical teacher, but he evidently knew what he was doing, because he was the only vocal teacher she had (except for her mother) in those formative years, and she learned a lot about voice production from him. Meanwhile, her work as a typist took her to several successive offices, mostly those of wholesalers of farm equipment. Joan was a lonely girl at this time, and she welcomed the severe schedule of working as a secretary in the daytime and practicing at night. She won some small prizes as a singer and gained confidence. When she was eighteen, she entered the *Sun* Aria Contest, an affair sponsored all over Australia by the

35

Sydney *Sun*. "It was something like the Metropolitan Opera Auditions of the Air," she recalled the other day. "But it was rather better, because you were not immediately typed as an opera singer, and you were not expected to do things that were beyond you. I entered the contest two years running without winning. Then I won the third year, got a prize, and was put on the radio for a broadcast." Finally, she decided to give up work as a typist and joined the Affiliated Music Clubs of New South Wales, which sent her on concert tours in small towns. Her big chance came when she entered what is known as the Mobil Quest, another vocal contest, sponsored by the Vacuum Oil Company. Here the stakes were bigger—a prize of one thousand pounds and the expectation of a trip to London or the Continent. Cousin John offered to contribute another thousand pounds if she won, and she did. London was the next step.

In the meantime, she had met Bonynge, who was a prize piano pupil at the local conservatory of music and had played at some of the concerts put on by the Affiliated Music Clubs. Bonynge had been a pupil of Lindley Evans, who had been Melba's last accompanist. He became a fine Chopin pianist. After his graduation, he went to London to take up a scholarship at the Royal College of Music; Joan sang at his going-away concert in Sydney. Bonynge, already a connoisseur of voices, thought that her voice was powerful, brilliant, and a bit inexpressive. By the time Joan got to London—properly accompanied by her mother—Bonynge had been there for a year. He was staying at a boardinghouse, living the life of a poor student. One of his friends was Terry McEwen, and both of them, according to McEwen, were record nuts. They used to visit each other to listen to recordings of great voices, and they began to develop theories about them. Bonynge loved voices with a passion known only to the confirmed opera buff. He was still studying the piano, but he spent all his spare time listening to voices and playing the deceptively simple accompaniments of bel-canto opera. "I think he was a frustrated prima donna," McEwen recently said. (Bonynge had once been a boy soprano.) Meanwhile, Joan and her mother rented a bed-sitting room, and since her mother was a very good cook, in a simple way, Bonynge often came to dinner, which was much better prepared than the dinners at his boardinghouse. At first, Mrs. Sutherland did not particularly like Bonynge. But Bonynge was intensely interested in Joan's voice, and it was not long before he was coaching her, even though she was studying at the Royal College of Music, where her teachers were bent on turning her huge voice into a Wagnerian soprano.

"Those first days in London were not a particularly hard time," Miss Sutherland has recalled. "But I didn't want to call on Cousin John again, and I wanted to be sure I had sufficient money to bridge the gap between those insecure early days and the possibility of getting into Covent Garden or going to the Continent to try my luck there, if I had to. Not having any foreign language I spoke very well, that was going to be a bit difficult. So we made ourselves a budget. I think that my mother was a little foolish about it. We could have spent a bit more money. I tried to convince her, but she was afraid. I thought it better to spend it in odd little ways, like going to the theater or making trips—to Windsor or Kew Gardens. I felt she was pennypinching a bit too much." But Bonynge continued to come to dinner. He didn't believe for a minute that Joan was a Wagnerian-type soprano, despite the power of her voice. The Sutherlands had bought a cheap piano, and on it Bonynge accompanied Joan in anything she wanted to sing, from vocalises to operatic roles. By now Bonynge had developed a secret ambition to turn her into a coloratura soprano. He taught her the florid aria "Qui la voce sua soave," from Bellini's *I Puritani*, and by the time she auditioned for Covent Garden she was able to sing a whole gamut of arias, ranging from Wagner to Bellini. The committee that auditioned her seemed to like her voice, but didn't seem to like her square-jawed looks, and told her to come back in six

Miss Sutherland as a child.

Miss Sutherland and her favorite conductor, her husband, Richard Bonynge.

Left: With her mother after a performance of *Lucia* at Covent Garden.

Miss Sutherland as Lucia in Donizetti's opera *Lucia di Lammermoor*.

Miss Sutherland as Marie in Donizetti's *La Fille du Régiment*, at the Metropolitan.

months. She auditioned three times before she was taken into the company, and when she was, in the fall of 1952, it was as one of Covent Garden's resident sopranos—available for almost any role—at about thirty dollars a week. She sang both Aida and the High Priestess in *Aida*. She sang Penelope Rich in Britten's *Gloriana*. She sang Amelia in *Un Ballo in Maschera;* Olympia, and then all three roles, in *The Tales of Hoffmann;* the First Rhinemaiden in *Das Rheingold* and *Götterdämmerung;* the Woodbird in *Siegfried;* Agathe in *Der Freischütz;* Eva in *Die Meistersinger;* Gilda in *Rigoletto;* the Countess in *Le Nozze di Figaro;* Pamina, the Queen of the Night, and the First Lady in *Die Zauberflöte;* and, finally, Desdemona to Ramón Vinay's Otello, which really put her on the map. She even sang the mezzo role of Brangäne in *Tristan und Isolde,* under Sir John Barbirolli's baton, while on tour in Manchester. (The scheduled Brangäne had fallen ill.) She did this role at Bonynge's suggestion. "I'm no mezzo-soprano," she had protested. But he had insisted, saying, "I'll teach you the role." "And he convinced me that I *did* know the role," she once recalled. "When I got out there, I did all right. Fortunately, the role is a short one." Perhaps most significantly, in view of her future career, she sang the small role of Clotilda in *Norma* in a historic performance in which the title role was sung by Maria Callas, while Ebe Stignani did the role of Adalgisa. Bonynge pointed out at this time that Callas had a large dramatic-soprano voice that had been trained to do the most complicated coloratura, and that Joan could do the same thing if she tried.

Meanwhile, Joan's mother had gone back to Australia to care for Joan's aunt, and Joan herself had moved to a comfortable house in Aubrey Walk, Notting Hill Gate. Bonynge moved in with her, and continued to bully her into singing bel canto. Shortly, they got married. The London climate was not good for her sinus and ear trouble. Doctors suggested all sorts of operations, but she maintained an attitude of stoicism and went on singing without them. She did Cleopatra in *Giulio Cesare* with the Handel Opera Society at Sadler's Wells, and Mozart's *Der Schauspieldirektor,* Donna Anna in *Don Giovanni,* the Countess in *Figaro,* and Elvira in *I Puritani* at Glyndebourne. But the directors there thought she was too big to sing Constanze in *The Abduction from the Seraglio.* "They had some idea that Constanze should be a petite type," she has said. Her teeth were giving her a lot of trouble at this time, and she finally agreed to have them capped. "She would spend four hours in a dentist's chair, and then sing gloriously at Covent Garden," McEwen recalls. Norman Ayrton, the drama coach, taught her how to move onstage. "Joan has always had the sort of personality that everyone wants to help," somebody has remarked with considerable acuteness. And help her everyone did. She made a trip to Vancouver to sing Donna Anna under the direction of the famous German *metteur en scène* Günther Rennert, and Mr. Rennert devoted almost all his time to her. The result was not only a vocal but a dramatic success.

Finally, in 1959, the administration at Covent Garden allowed her to do *Lucia* in the original language. Curiously, it was the first time *Lucia* had been done in London in seventy years, except for one performance by Toti dal Monte in 1925. It was a big occasion. Tullio Serafin, the most noted of all Italian opera conductors, was the maestro, and the designer-director was Franco Zeffirelli. "Zeffirelli worked hard with her," McEwen remembers, "and at last he even convinced her that she could be a beautiful woman." This *Lucia* was a landmark. Both Callas and Schwarzkopf attended the dress rehearsal. Serafin had advised Joan to save her voice by singing softly at this rehearsal, but, knowing that these two famous prima donnas were in the audience, she could not resist showing the full power and brilliance of her singing. After her first aria, the members of the orchestra—somewhat to the discomfiture of the two divas in the theater, it may be supposed—unexpectedly put down their instruments and applauded her, and after the Mad Scene even the chorus onstage shouted bravos. At the opening performance that night, the London critics raved. A soprano superstar had been discovered, and it was not long before Joan Sutherland was in fervent demand on the Continent and in America.

Since that *Lucia,* Miss Sutherland has been singing at La Scala, at the Vienna and Paris Operas, at the Chicago and Dallas and San Francisco Operas, and, of course, at Covent Garden, in addition to spending several months each year in New York singing at the Met. Like most soprano superstars, she has cut down her repertory and become a specialist. Her principal roles now are in the operas *Norma, I Puritani, The Tales of Hoffmann, Giulio Cesare, Semiramide, Lucrezia Borgia, La Sonnambula, Lucia,* and *Maria Stuarda*—all of them bel-canto works—and when she added Donizetti's *La Fille du Régiment,* her first comic role, she enjoyed a huge success at the Metropolitan. Miss Sutherland, who is basically a jolly soul, approached this role with gusto, and in performing it she uses one of her minor, but appropriate, talents— that for making faces. She has been making faces off the stage for some time, and McEwen says that her grotesque expressions have often lightened recording sessions by breaking people up and thus relaxing them. She also added Gilda in *Rigoletto* to her repertory at the Met, but, though she could do it with ease, she did not sing the high note at the end of "Caro nome" that most sopranos try to knock their audiences out with. Verdi wrote a long trill for the end of the aria—the high note was added later by some soprano—and that is enough for Miss Sutherland.

Bonynge, of course, realized a long time ago that he was riding the tail of a comet. He is a selfless man, deeply devoted to his wife's voice. But references to him as "Mr. Sutherland" got under his skin, and so he decided to become a conductor. He was encouraged in this move by McEwen, Geraldine Souvaine (of the Metropolitan's Saturday-afternoon broadcasts), and Ann Colbert, the impresario who is the Bonynges' manager. He made his first appearance as a conductor at a concert in Rome in 1962, and since then he has conducted practically all the operas Miss Sutherland has appeared in. He has studied with Tullio Serafin and has been given pointers on conducting by Henry Lewis, Marilyn Horne's husband and the conductor of the New Jersey Symphony Orchestra. Miss Sutherland is very loyal to her husband as a conductor. Once, in Hamburg, he was hissed, and she thereupon refused to take any curtain calls. "For me, he is the perfect conductor," she once explained. "He knows how to allow for breathing, and he has a complete knowledge of how I feel and what I am capable of. He has the knack of drawing a good performance out of me. Everyone asks about this incredible knack he has with singing and singers. I don't know where it comes from. Often, he'll hear someone sing and make a snap decision and say, 'I'd love to hear him or her sing such-and-such a role.' And they get the chance later on, and it's a great success. He seems to react instinctively, and, of course, he has a certain knowledge, too."

One day Miss Sutherland remarked, "I think *Norma* is the most womanly opera I sing," the adjective "womanly" saying a great deal about the way she thinks of herself. She has no desire, for example, to sing Cherubini's opera *Medea,* which is about a woman who kills her children and which requires a sort of strenuous singing that she finds uncongenial. She is extremely feminine, down-to-earth, and sensible in her attitude toward her art. Her opinions about the so-called golden age of singing, in the eighteenth and early nineteenth century (from which her own repertoire comes), are not entirely flattering. "I think there were a lot of vulgarities that crept in," she said. "I don't mean holding notes too long and that sort of thing—I'm a great noteholder myself, and I don't think I'm vulgar—but some of the ornamentation of the golden age was excessive. People walked in and out of the registers of the voice. There was a lot of indiscriminate gear changing. Breaking the registers as it used to be done is exciting, but I don't like to do it, because when I do, I feel that it is damaging my voice production. I don't think that too much of it is good for the voice." (All voices are divided into "registers"—head, middle, and chest. The average person can recognize these registers when he yodels; yodeling is deliberately crossing the breaks between head and chest registers. It is not thought nowadays to be good for professional singers.)

And what does Miss Sutherland think about subjects like religion, life, death, and eternity? She is at no loss for an answer. "I don't know what to call religious. We were brought up very strictly—went to church twice or three times a day. I am very glad I had that sort of background, because I think that one has to have some sort of faith to hang on to. I've been taught to believe in an afterlife. I think it's very interesting. I sometimes wonder whether one who has got so much out of life *deserves* an afterlife." And is she superstitious? "Well, no. I have various sorts of good-luck charms that people have given me. I would never go onstage without putting them on my dressing table—a funny little frog, full of dried peas, I think, with a toweling sort of body. Then, I have a bear that was given me by the man who takes care of my costumes. And, of course, there's a little Madonna of Montserrat that I was given in Barcelona by the woman who dressed me. I used to bring one red rose for that Madonna before each performance. But I'm not really superstitious, or particularly sympathetic to the Catholic Church. I confess that I've done some performances without bringing a rose for the Madonna, and even some without taking the Madonna out of the bag."

At present, her chief worry is how to cope with the enormous number of offers she receives and still retain the two and a half months of lesiure that she considers indispensable at her home in Switzerland. "I practice during that period, though," she said not long ago. "Sometimes I learn new roles. I haven't had a chance to let my voice rest in the last three years. One hankers after the metropolis, of course. But there are times when I want to get away from it all. At least, in Switzerland one doesn't have the tension of continuous travel. And when I'm there, I don't sing every day. I may sing one day, study the words next day, and so on. But I just don't have the time to fit everything in. The recording companies want me when I'm available, and the summertime, when the opera season is over, is the time when they expect me to record. Then you have to be strong and say, 'I don't intend to fill any engagements until November,' if you really want to have a break. It's very hard to allocate your time evenly. They want us to go to Hamburg. But I don't see how we can. It would be good to have a shorter planning schedule—a short period at the Met, and so on. But then there's San Francisco. I've already signed up for the next three years. I suppose that one should feel gratified that one is still going strong, without the feeling that one is just scratching around. On the other hand, it's very difficult to say no."

Apprehensions about going downhill, now that she is at the top? "Every time you sing, this occurs to you. There are people out there wondering when you are going to topple. I think I have a reasonably healthy attitude about that, because after you have been trekking around the world to rented apartments or hotels, wondering about the weather, catching the next plane—when you do this perpetually for twenty years you have to be prepared for just such a thing. I was not a very ambitious person. People have treated me wonderfully. I've had a marvelous career. I was ambitious enough to leave Australia and try to get into Covent Garden. I suppose that this was because of Cousin John and the rest. It wasn't just the relatives, either. I suppose I wouldn't have entered the competitions in Australia if I hadn't been aiming at something a little above the average." A little above the average.

Photograph by Louis Mélançon

Miss Horne as Adalgisa in Bellini's *Norma*.

II
Marilyn Horne

Marilyn Horne with her husband, Henry Lewis, the conductor of the New Jersey Symphony.

Terry McEwen, who is a frustrated tenor as well as the manager of the classical division of London Records, and who presumably knows a good deal about singers, once remarked that although Joan Sutherland was, in his opinion, the world's greatest singer, the world's greatest voice belonged to Marilyn Horne. Allowing for the possible exaggeration that always attaches to the term "world's greatest" and for possible prejudice on Mr. McEwen's part (he records both singers), most concert- and operagoers would agree with him. Miss Horne has a voice of almost incredible power and range, and long training has made it into one of the most technically efficient instruments in the history of singing. As great singers go, she is young, being just thirty-eight (most great singers are great between the ages of thirty-five and fifty), and she may be regarded as being at her peak, or rapidly approaching it. Her voice is remarkable for its quality throughout its enormous range, which includes areas ordinarily patrolled by contraltos, mezzo-sopranos, and dramatic sopranos, and for its agility and accuracy. Its texture is warm—powerful at the bottom and brilliant at the top—and her way of using it often reminds one of a skillful skier rushing down slopes, making spectacular jumps, and always landing with absolute accuracy. Her range permits her to sing every kind of music and to play every kind of role—all the way from the timid Mimi of *La Bohème*, through the most exacting parts of the bel-canto repertory, to the thundering notes of Wagner's Brünnhilde. So far, she has not specialized, and there is considerable speculation among opera buffs as to just which way she will finally go. Even Miss Horne herself is not quite sure. She has billed herself as a mezzo-soprano, but in the programs of several New York recitals she has called herself a soprano, and proved it by singing a number of unquestionably soprano arias. Besides being able to sing almost anything in the operatic repertory, she is a very quick study. Kurt Herbert Adler, the general director of the San Francisco Opera, once said, "You don't ask what the role is. You ask if Marilyn is available. She can learn a part quicker than almost anyone I've ever seen."

Miss Horne's career has been stunning. Her American debut—with the San Francisco Opera in 1960—was in the soprano role of Marie in Alban Berg's bitterly realistic opera *Wozzeck*, a role she repeated later at Covent Garden. Shortly afterward, she embarked on the most florid of coloratura roles, usually singing with Joan Sutherland and helping her bring back the almost forgotten bel-canto operas of the early nineteenth century. She did the role of Arsace in Rossini's *Semiramide* under the direction of Sarah Caldwell in Boston in 1965, and did it again, to enormous ovations, at the Chicago Opera. There was also a series of *Normas* with Miss Sutherland. First, the opera was done for the Vancouver Opera Association, in 1963. Then it was recorded for RCA-Victor, followed by two seasons at Covent Garden. Finally, in March, 1970, it reached the Metropolitan, and, though the staging left something to be desired, the singing of Miss Sutherland and Miss Horne was generally regarded as brilliant. (After one performance, Rudolf Bing, the general manager of the Met, called up Miss Horne at home and said that he wanted her to sing the role of

Rosina in *The Barber of Seville* at the Met the next June. She replied that she was already under contract for that month. "What's a contract?" said Mr. Bing jocularly. "It's a contract with *Covent Garden*," Miss Horne said. "What's Covent Garden?" Mr. Bing went on in the same vein. "Oh," said Miss Horne, realizing that she was getting nowhere, "it's a place where I sell fruits and vegetables." Later, she said to a friend, "Mr. Bing does so like to be funny.") Additionally, over the past eleven years, Miss Horne has appeared (with Beverly Sills) as Néoclès in Rossini's *The Siege of Corinth* at La Scala; in the same composer's *The Barber of Seville* at the Chicago Opera; in Meyerbeer's *Le Prophète* (an opera that is almost unheard today because of its difficulty) on the Italian radio; in Bellini's *I Capuletti ed i Montecchi* at Carnegie Hall; and in practically all the recently revived bel-canto operas. She has also recorded, for London Records, the mezzo role in Donizetti's *Anna Bolena*, the title role in Gluck's *Orfeo*, and the lyric soprano role of Zerlina in Mozart's *Don Giovanni*. And she has sung Brünnhilde's immolation scene from *Götterdämmerung* with the Boston Symphony, the Los Angeles Philharmonic, and the Philadelphia Orchestra. The point of all this is that these roles are among the most difficult in opera—some wildly ornate, others powerful and sustained—and that for Miss Horne they constituted a collective challenge that she accepted and brought off with something very near vocal perfection. By the time she made her Metropolitan debut, in *Norma*, Miss Horne was already known throughout the operatic world as one of its most extraordinary virtuosos.

Miss Horne, owing to a rather peculiar set of circumstances that, at first, seemed to have little to do with her vocal ability, opened the 1972-73 season at the Metropolitan Opera House in the title role of a new production of *Carmen*. It was not a role that she was famous for, though she had sung it, having dubbed the part for Dorothy Dandridge in the movie *Carmen Jones* very early in her career and having sung the real thing in San Francisco in 1961, in Philadelphia the following year, and in a production by Sarah Caldwell in Boston in 1968, after which she had vowed never to sing it again because she thought it was not ideally suited to her voice. But the circumstances of her opening at the Met were dictated by an extraneous influence—namely, that of Rudolf Bing, who had had control of the casting for what was to have been the late Goeran Gentele's first season as the new general director. He had cast Miss Horne and the forceful tenor James McCracken—two singers hardly anybody could imagine on the same stage—for Mr. Gentele's opening night and suggested that Mr. Gentele open with *Tannhäuser*, which Mr. Bing knew very well was the dowdiest and most moth-eaten production in the Metropolitan's repertory. Mr. Gentele wasn't having any of it. He had seen it. But he was stuck with Mr. Bing's all but insoluble casting combination. He had one of the most powerful tenors alive, plus one of the most powerful and agile sopranos, whose agility would have been completely wasted in *Tannhäuser*. It must have been an agonizing moment, but Mr. Gentele rose to the problem gallantly. He decided to do a new production of *Carmen* with the original spoken dialogue instead of the customary recitatives that were written by Ernest Guiraud after Bizet's death. And Mr. Gentele proposed to direct the production himself.

Then, tragically, Mr. Gentele was killed in an automobile accident in Sardinia, leaving the Met not only without a permanent general manager, but also without a director for the opening *Carmen*. His successor, Schuyler Chapin, wisely turned the job of directing the production over to Bodo Igesz, an excellent man who had been languishing in the ranks of the assistant directors and who promised to follow Mr. Gentele's detailed notes on the production as closely as possible. The sets and costumes had been designed by Josef Svoboda under Mr. Gentele's supervision. There was considerable speculation among opera buffs as to what would happen on this bedeviled opening night. Everybody knew that Miss Horne could toss off the vocal aspects of Carmen with no trouble at all, but would she make a great Carmen as an actress? Would Mr. McCracken, one of the most powerful of tenors, exhibit the lyricism and the combination of tenderness and fury that the role of Don José demands? Would Mr. Igesz be able to modify the talents of both artists so that a believable whole would be achieved? If so, he would have produced a miracle.

When the Met finally opened, the speculation seemed idle. The miracle occurred. The scenery and costumes by Mr. Svoboda were a knockout. Miss Horne, though her movements onstage were a bit reserved, proved to be a sensation. Critics compared her Carmen with that of the celebrated Bruna Castagna, the great Carmen of Edward Johnson's regime at the Met. It was magnificently sung and acted with temperament and even a touch of humor. As for Mr. McCracken it was obvious that Mr. Gentele had had extraordinary intuition in fitting the role to him. He proved to be a Don José of such vocal mastery that he sang the last note of the famous "Flower Song" pianissimo—a trick that few tenors of modern times have been able to bring off. Everybody agreed that Miss Horne had reached a peak in her career and that the Met had acquired its greatest Carmen in thirty years.

Offstage, Miss Horne is a robust woman, standing about five feet two and a half inches, with dark-brown hair, blue eyes, naturally pink cheeks, and an air of blooming health and vitality. She wears glasses practically everywhere she goes, often a pair of gold-rimmed grannies. She is forceful ("I am more apt to swear than cry," she says of herself); extremely ambitious to set new records as a singer; a bit aggressive in her relations with any singer other than Miss Sutherland, whom she admires to the point of idolatry; and possessed of an enormous fund of good humor and spirit. She has a tireless interest in new or unfamiliar operas (she thinks Tchaikovsky's *Joan of Arc,* which almost nobody has even heard of in recent years, is a great opera and should be produced), a go-ahead-and-hang-the-difficulties attitude toward her work, and an absolute independence of opinion, public or otherwise.

One instance of this independence is that Miss Horne is married to a black man—Henry Lewis, the conductor of the New Jersey Symphony. Mr. Lewis took over this assignment after a distinguished career as a guest conductor and then assistant conductor of the Los Angeles Philharmonic under Zubin Mehta. A Californian by birth, Mr. Lewis founded his own orchestra there— the Los Angeles Chamber Orchestra—and in 1963 took it, along with Miss Horne, on a successful State Department-sponsored tour of Europe. In his present post, Mr. Lewis has made the New Jersey Symphony not only a fine orchestra but an exceptionally well-trained one. He also serves as Miss Horne's coach, and advises her on musical matters. The Lewises live in an upper-class section of Orange, New Jersey, in a pleasant house that looks as if it had come straight out of *House Beautiful*. Even the lawn and trees surrounding the house look as though they had been ordered from a catalogue, and the garden is manicured as only a professional can manicure it. All this indicates that the Lewises haven't time to bother with their own gardening or decorating, which is easy to believe, since both are busy artists, often on the road. The Lewises have a very intelligent seven-year-old daughter named Angela. Like all children of busy artists, Angela is the source of considerable worry to her parents. Mr. Lewis, a tall, rather handsome man, has to do a good deal of socializing with the people in his musical parish, and Miss Horne, of course, is often on the road or abroad. The family is to all appearances a close and happy one, but Miss Horne, who is known at home as Jackie, is conscious of the currently irreconcilable rift between career and motherhood, and she hopes that Angela is getting enough affection.

Miss Horne made her New York debut on February 21, 1961, in an American Opera Society concert performance of Bellini's

Beatrice di Tenda. It happened also to be the New York debut of Joan Sutherland. Nearly everybody agreed that the evening as a whole was a fine one, and, from a vocal point of view, a sensation. Next day, Miss Horne and her husband bought all the papers. Mr. Lewis began to read the *Times* review out loud. "Don't read the whole thing," Miss Horne said. "Just the part about me." Mr. Lewis scanned the review and discovered that there was nothing for him to read; the *Times* reviewer had become so carried away by Miss Sutherland that he had written simply, "The other members of the cast fell down."

Speaking of the incident the other day, Miss Horne said, "I don't think I cried. But it sure was a disenchanting experience." Her husband said, "Mademoiselle Horne never cries. But Jackie Lewis sometimes does."

Jackie is a name that has stuck to Miss Horne ever since childhood; when she was born, her older brother, Richard, who had wanted her to be a boy, insisted on the nickname. The family was a fairly large one—two boys and two girls. Jackie was born in Bradford, Pennsylvania, in 1934, of German, Swedish, and Dutch stock. Her father, Bentz Horne, who died in 1956, made a not very lavish living as Bradford's tax assessor and, on Sundays, as a tenor in many of the local churches. He was much more interested in singing than in tax assessing, and from the beginning he was determined that Marilyn should become a singer. He gave her her first lessons, and throughout his life he encouraged and scolded her by turns. She became a professional at the age of four, when she sang "Believe Me, If All Those Endearing Young Charms" at a picnic in Bradford to promote the reelection of Franklin Delano Roosevelt; her fee was a lime soda pop. She also studied with a local teacher named Hazel Bittenbender, who, according to Miss Horne, sang out of one side of her mouth, causing her pupil to wonder if that was the proper way to sing. In her subsequent studies with the head of a local choir, she learned that that was *not* the proper way to sing. Then, as her voice improved, she studied with Miss Edna Luce, for whom she has great respect to this day. From her she learned how a singer should breathe, and she still breathes that way. Miss Luce made her stand up straight—stomach muscles drawn tight—and inflate her lungs without letting her chest or shoulders rise. It sounds very simple, but it is not. "Ninety percent of what's wrong with singers today is that they don't breathe right," Miss Horne states authoritatively. On the other hand, she does not think that female singers should be taught as early as she was. "Vocal training for women shouldn't begin until adolescence," she says. "It's different with men. Many fine tenors and basses began as choirboys."

When she was eleven, Bentz Horne decided to move his family to southern California in order to take advantage of the superior educational system there, and the family has been California-based ever since. At the time, it consisted of Bentz himself, who continued his work as a church singer in Long Beach, where they settled; his wife, Bernice (now an executive with Invacare, a hospital-supply manufacturing company); Miss Horne's older sister, Gloria (now married to a Mexican-American named Jack Palacios, who is associate conductor of the Long Beach Symphony); Richard (now an assistant superintendent of the Los Angeles County schools); and a younger brother, Jay (a college student and part-time rock singer). It was just after the Second World War when the Hornes made their move, and housing in Long Beach was almost nonexistent; Miss Horne remembers that the family lived for a time in a single room. She continued her vocal instruction and was soon singing in the William Ripley Dorr Choir of St. Luke's Episcopal Church, a locally distinguished group. Then she attended junior high school in Long Beach, where she occasionally played football with the boys. Her love of football continued for quite some time, and often led to considerable frustration: she couldn't yell with the crowd for fear of damaging her voice. In 1951, she got a scholarship at the University of Southern California. There she found a gifted vocal teacher—William Vennard, a bass with a thorough knowledge of how voices are produced. "He was a shy, rather uncommunicative man, but he was a great teacher, and especially good for me, because he encouraged experimentation," she remarked. "I would come to him saying, 'I was fooling around with this, and look what happened,' and then I'd sing the passage for him. Instead of bawling me out, he'd encourage me." At that time, she was also singing with the Roger Wagner Chorale, the finest chorus in Los Angeles, which was used by the Los Angeles Philharmonic and by other distinguished orchestras. (She doesn't recommend this sort of choral work for anyone who is interested in a solo career, however. Her powerful voice had a way of standing out, and that wasn't good for the chorus' balance and smoothness.) She remained with the Chorale until 1954, when her career as a recitalist really began. "Otherwise, I was just having a good time, dating and going to parties," she has said. "My father was continually saying that I would never make anything of myself. He seemed to be convinced of it. But now I know that he was just putting pressure on me." At the age of twenty, she appeared in a recital at the Hollywood Bowl, and her father picked a fight with her beforehand. "He did this just to get the adrenalin flowing," she has said. "All he wanted was for me to be a great singer."

Meanwhile, at the University of Southern California things were happening that pointed toward the future. The celebrated German operatic director and actor Carl Ebert had settled in southern California and was head of the opera department at the university. Ebert, who had a lifetime of opera directing and acting behind him, was a first-rate instructor, and Miss Horne's memories of him are wildly enthusiastic. "Oh, wow!" she exclaimed the other day. "He was a terrific man, a great actor. I wasn't really in a position to assimilate what a man like that had to offer. I wish I were working

Miss Horne as Carmen in the Metropolitan's new production of Bizet's opera.

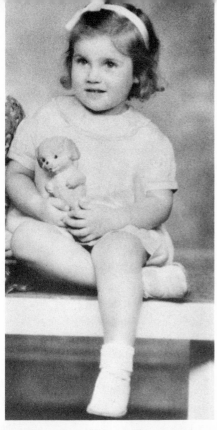

Left: Miss Horne as a child.

Below: As Neocles in Rossini's *Siege of Corinth*.

Photograph by David H. Fishman
Miss Horne as Rosina in Rossini's *The Barber of Seville*.

Miss Horne (*right*) as the Babylonian general Arsace in a scene from the rarely produced Rossini opera *Semiramide*. Joan Sutherland (*left*) sings the title role.

Photograph by Louis Mélançon

Miss Horne as Adalgisa in the Vancouver Opera's production of *Norma*.

with him now. He was extraordinary-looking—blue eyes, white hair. A former matinee idol. Women swooned over him. When he did Hamlet, the ladies used to die." Under Ebert's direction, she appeared with the Guild Opera Company, a professional troupe, playing Hansel in *Hansel and Gretel* and Hata in *The Bartered Bride* (both mezzo roles), and, finally, the lead in Rossini's *La Cenerentola* (a contralto role requiring enormous agility). "That was the first coloratura role I ever sang," she has said. "I didn't know I was a coloratura. I knew I could sing all those notes, all right, but I didn't realize that there was anything special about it. In fact, my father always said that you weren't a singer at all unless you had that sort of agility." Ebert apparently realized that there was something special about her ability to sing all those notes, and he advised her to go to Europe to continue her studies. Miss Horne determined that she would—as soon as she could. It was at about this time that she got the job of dubbing the voice of Carmen for Dorothy Dandridge. Actually, she had auditioned for a job in the chorus of the movie, singing the lyric-soprano role of Micaela as a sample of her talent. "I can sing low, too," she assured her auditors, and she showed them. As a result, she was elevated from the chorus to Carmen herself. "For the movie, I tried to sing more like a movie actress than an opera singer," she recalls. Meanwhile, she was singing as a soloist in oratorios and operas around Los Angeles, and had acquired a manager, Dorothy Huttenback, who has remained a lifelong friend. She was also studying repertoire— recital, not opera—with Gwendolyn Koldofsky, the widow of Adolph Koldofsky, a well-known violinist who had specialized in the works of Schoenberg. Mrs. Koldofsky finally sent her to study with Lotte Lehmann, in Santa Barbara, and it was with Miss Lehmann that she learned the subtleties of lieder singing. "Lehmann opened up the whole world of what imagination can do for a singer," she says. "She has an almost childish imagination.

65

Recently, a critic accused me of trying to portray a different role in each song in a recital. That's exactly what I *was* trying to do. That was Lehmann."

Earlier, Miss Horne had appeared as a soloist at Robert Craft's famous Monday Evening Concerts in Los Angeles, at which more music by Stravinsky was played than was being heard anywhere else. Through these concerts she met Stravinsky himself, as well as his close friend Aldous Huxley. "Imagine!" she said recently. "There I was, nineteen years old and having dinner with Stravinsky and Huxley! All I remember is Huxley talking a lot about Gesualdo, a sixteenth-century Italian prince who was famous not only as a composer but as a murderer and all-round criminal." Once, she discovered Stravinsky and Huxley bent over the keyboard of a piano solemnly trying to decipher what to them was a highly mysterious inscription. They were looking at a sign that said "No Cotton-Pickin' Drinks on This Instrument," and they were relieved when she explained what it meant.

It was during her days at the University of Southern California that she met her future husband. Lewis' father was an automobile dealer in Los Angeles, and his mother was a nurse, who eventually became an administrator and a teacher of nurses at Queen of Angels Hospital in that city. Henry Lewis was a bass player with the Los Angeles Philharmonic, and he played in the orchestra for the performance of *The Bartered Bride* in which Miss Horne sang. He noticed the power of her lower voice; in fact, he whispered to a colleague, "Who's that tenor up there?" After the performance, he met the tenor, and wheels started turning. Mr. Lewis, who is two years older than Miss Horne, turned out to be more than a bass player. Drafted into the Army in 1955, he was sent to Stuttgart, where he soon took over the conductorship of the Seventh Army Symphony, a servicemen's group, and he gained much experience with it. The great Dutch conductor Eduard van Beinum heard him conduct and began to take an interest in him. When Lewis got out of the Army and returned to the Los Angeles Philharmonic, van Beinum himself was in charge of the orchestra, and he encouraged Lewis to found the Los Angeles Chamber Orchestra, with which Lewis made his State Department tour of Europe. Van Beinum also allowed him to conduct a number of the Philharmonic's concerts and to take over the orchestra's weekly Symphonies for Youth concerts. By the time Lewis married Miss Horne, he was well on the road to professional conductorship.

Miss Horne's family was not very enthusiastic about her friendship with Mr. Lewis. And her father was not at all enthusiastic about her idea of going to Europe to study. Bentz Horne was something of a chauvinist. American singers, he thought, should do all their studying in this country; European music had dried up. But Miss Horne had already found her independence of spirit, and she was determined to go. So she did, in the fall of 1956. After a stopover at the Venice Biennale, she spent a year in Vienna, studying operatic repertoire with one of the coaches of the State Opera and learning German at the same time. She wouldn't allow anybody to touch her vocal production; Vennard had taught her well, and her opinion of Austrian vocal teachers was not high. Then she got a job in Germany with the Gelsenkirchen Municipal Opera. Gelsenkirchen is a smoky town in the Ruhr Valley with a population of about half a million, but, like many German towns, it has a pretty good opera company, and the experience of singing a large number of roles there (even though everything was sung in German) was valuable. Among her roles were Mimi in *La Bohème*, Minnie in *Fanciulla del West*, Tatiana in *Eugene Onegin* and Amelia in *Simon Boccanegra*. Today she remembers Gelsenkirchen both critically and gratefully. "That kind of an opera company can breed mediocrity, but it was a good place to start," she remarked. "You have to know exactly what you want out of your career. If you want to be a star, you don't bother with other things. While I was at Gelsenkirchen, I found out for the first time what human beings are really all about. The general director was an ex-singer and a wonderful man. But he was also an ex-Nazi, and had held a contract under Hitler—a lifetime contract. He was jailed after the war, but he had been released by the time I got there, and was back at his old stand. We had many conversations about Nazism, and all this talk about race made me realize even more strongly that people everywhere have prejudices. I finally got up the courage to marry Henry."

The Lewises were married on July 2, 1960, in Los Angeles under rather stormy circumstances. Mr. Wagner, of the Wagner Chorale, prophesied that her career would be ruined. Her mother refused to attend the ceremony. "Of course, in Bradford, where Mother came from, we had even looked down on the Italians and Irish. By the time I was married, my experience of the world was much greater than Mother's. My parents had always talked tolerance, but talking and taking a step like mine were pretty different. Mother went all to pieces. I cried a lot." Within a few weeks, however, Mrs. Horne relented, and she is now very fond of Lewis.

The human voice—particularly the female voice—is a delicate instrument, easily disturbed by the ills of the flesh and, in some ways, not ideally built for the more complex types of singing. It commonly falls into three (some theorists say two) registers, which are determined by the muscular settings of the vocal cords. Generally, the lower, or "chest," register and the top, or "head," register are the best naturally developed areas of the range. Between them lies the middle register (which is treated by the two-register theorists as a mere link between chest and head tones), and at the top of this there are a few so-called "passage notes" leading up to the head register. It often happens that the middle register is the weak part of a singer's range and that the passage notes just above it are even weaker. Between the registers there can be a sort of break, or yodel. Naturally, a great deal of vocal training is devoted to bridging the breaks and to strengthening the middle voice—especially the passage notes—to give a smooth, seamless quality to the entire range. By a certain physiological adjustment, a given register can be expanded upward or downward by a few notes, but the practice is not universally considered healthy for the voice. Some singers never really succeed in strengthening the middle voice and the passage notes, and one can detect this fact at many an opera performance. Miss Horne's middle voice is remarkably well handled, giving her a seemingly flawless range from the chest tones to head tones. Her chest tones are among the most powerful to be heard anywhere today—"When I open up down there, you'd better look out," she has said—and her head tones are extremely brilliant and agile. But bringing all this range into an equality of sound has taken some doing. The powerful chest tones have had to be restrained. The middle voice has been strengthened, but until two years ago the passage notes were still something of a problem, since this is the last part of the voice to develop. For her, the passage notes are E, F, and G at the top of the staff. From there, her middle register descends to somewhere around E flat at the bottom of the staff, and from there on down to F sharp the powerful chest tones take over.

Miss Horne is of the opinion that Giuseppe Verdi wrote badly for the voice. "He wrote for dramatic reasons, and he has a way of hammering at the weakest spot in a singer's range," she says. "When a young person sings Azucena [in *Il Trovatore*], for example, it's very bad for the voice. Amneris [in *Aida*] gets a gorgeous aria to sing, and then comes the judgment scene, and that is terrible. You can't sing these roles in your twenties." What Miss Horne means is that Verdi's roles are not right for *her* type of voice, which is a bel-canto instrument, better attuned to Rossini, Donizetti, and Bellini. In order to sing Verdi's soprano or mezzo-soprano roles (the roles just mentioned are both mezzo), she has to bring her chest register up to tackle those passage notes a good deal of the time. This is extremely awkward for her. She sang Eboli in *Don Carlo* in San Francisco, for example, without any outstanding success, because her voice is simply not suited to the role, though she managed to make a success of it later in San Antonio. Verdi wrote for a different kind of singer: a lyric soprano of the type best exemplified by Leontyne Price, who has no trouble at all with Verdi roles; in fact, she thinks that Verdi wrote better for the voice than anybody except perhaps Mozart.

Nevertheless, in the kind of music she sings best, Miss Horne has remarkable smoothness throughout her enormous range, and she works hard to retain it. Though her voice has been compared with that of Rosa Ponselle, and she herself is inclined to compare it with that of the late Ernestine Schumann-Heink ("Schumann-Heink had a brilliant and very loud upper register, and so have I"), she always thinks of Lilli Lehmann, an incredibly versatile singer of the last decades of the nineteenth century, when she feels overworked. "Lilli Lehmann was a terrific worker—a real *Kraft-durch-Freude* type," she says. "When I'm feeling sorry for myself, I think of her." Miss Horne is a pronounced extrovert. Colds don't bother her; she has often sung with one. "We singers have good days and bad days, good weeks and bad weeks," she said recently. "The air pollution in New York is very bad for my throat. I use steam to counteract it. Singers always latch on to anything around in the way of cold prevention. The voice is something that is here today and gone tomorrow."

Like most singers, Miss Horne loves her work, loves to show off her voice, and loves audiences who appreciate her singing, and she is not above what sometimes amount to vocal circus tricks in order to impress such audiences. The most famous of these tricks (which are called for in certain bel-canto arias) is to take an enormous skip from the top of her range to her chest register, hitting the lower note, perhaps an octave and a half down, squarely and never off pitch. "You'd better know where the note *is*," she says. "If you don't, everything will come apart." Some of the real pleasure of listening to a Horne recital lies in such demonstrations of virtuosity, which have little to do with the music but a great deal to do with the art of vocalism. Critics have referred to Miss Horne as a showoff. But the fact is that she has something well worth showing off.

Miss Horne is not exactly an intellectual singer. Her attitude toward roles is far from the scholarly one of many prominent artists. "I read biography a great deal," she says, "but I wonder how valid that is. Some of the points are so subtle that I wonder how you can get them across to an audience. Besides, bel-canto opera doesn't necessarily stick very close to history where detail is concerned. Also, I wonder how important it is for you to know all the other roles in an opera. I always suspect people who say, 'I know every note and every word of everybody else's part.' Of course, after you have rehearsed enough, you get to know all the other roles anyway. But I never *try* to learn all the roles in any opera. I have enough trouble learning my own." On the other hand, Miss Horne pays great attention to the words she *is* singing, and, unlike some other singers, she is always distinct and understandable. "I keep the larynx down," she says. "I feel the words. The minute I get in front of an audience, something clicks and the diction comes out." On the subject of singing, she knows exactly what she wants and exactly how to get it. Unlike most contemporary sopranos, who regard Maria Callas as the greatest of modern models, she claims to have been equally influenced by Miss Callas and Joan Sutherland.

Lately, Miss Horne has become a little bored with the bel-canto repertoire, and in concerts she has turned increasingly to lieder or to song cycles by Mahler or to the repertoire of French songs. She has recorded Wagner's *Wesendonck Songs* and Mahler's *Kindertotenlieder* on a record that won the French Grand Prix du Disque in 1971. Her German is virtually perfect, learned in

Vienna and Gelsenkirchen, and her French is nearly as good. Her Italian, learned very early and polished through many visits to Italy, is excellent. She is a natural mimic, and this fact has helped her with languages. It has also helped her musical style; her musicianship—meaning all the details of phraseology and accentuation—is practically flawless. Like all singers of operatic caliber, she cannot hear her voice as others hear it, and she has to have her accompanist, Martin Katz, listen to her and advise her. Essentially, opera singers feel themselves sing rather than hear themselves. This is one of the peculiarities of the craft. That buzzing feeling in the head and chest is what they have to go by. "If you start listening to yourself, you're in trouble," Miss Horne has said. Her approach to a recital or an operatic performance is aggressive and sure. As Mr. Lewis says, "Jackie puts on her armor and pulls out her sword and sings." If things don't go right, she brazens them out. Her memory is not infallible. She has been known (infrequently) to forget whole phrases, but she has always managed to cover up any awkward moment. She has a totally devil-may-care approach to performances. For instance, she doesn't mind in the least when people in the audience smuggle in tape recorders, hoping to make bootleg records. When she notices someone with an attaché case (which is almost sure to contain a tape recorder) in his lap, she is as apt as not to wink at him or to wigwag to him from the stage, letting him know that she is quite aware of what he is doing. After all, she herself knows most of the tricks of the recording business. In Los Angeles, she at one time worked for a recording company that specialized in duplicating the big hits of well-known popular singers of the day, but with cheaper, unknown talent. Miss Horne contributed note-for-note replicas of Kay Starr's "Wheel of Fortune" and Peggy Lee's "Lover," and they did very well on the cut-rate shelves of the Los Angeles supermarkets. What a copy of one of them would be worth today is an interesting question.

At home, when she has the time, Miss Horne loves to cook, some of her favorite recipes being quiche Lorraine, gazpacho, and various cakes and pies. Generally, she sleeps well; if she doesn't, she reads. "But if it's something good, I get excited about it, and that doesn't help me a bit," she says. "The thing to do is to get an opera score and read *that*. That will bore you to death." She vocalizes (sings scales and arpeggios) for ten minutes to half an hour before performances, in order to warm up. She never touches alcohol, believing it to be very bad for the voice. She almost never suffers from nerves at a performance, though she admits that she was scared before her first New York recital when she saw the huge lines at a neighboring box office waiting for tickets to a Horowitz concert. One of her favorite pastimes has always been mimicking other singers and famous people in the musical world (*vide* Kay Starr and Peggy Lee). Today, her chief victims are Elisabeth Schwarzkopf (whose elegant singing style verges on self-caricature and is eminently mimicable), Miss Sutherland, and Louis Armstrong.

At the moment, Miss Horne's repertoire sprawls over nearly the whole literature of music for the voice. She is terribly ambitious to sing all the roles and all the lieder she can lay her hands on, and her husband encourages her. But this situation won't last. Eventually, like all star vocalists, she will specialize. This is not only because the repertoire of a star vocalist becomes limited to those roles in which she is most in demand—and there are only a certain number of performances that a singer can take part in in a given year—but also because the voice becomes accustomed to a particular kind of singing and cannot shift gears easily after a certain age. But which way will she go? Richard Bonynge, Joan Sutherland's husband, who is a dedicated promoter of bel-canto opera, wants her to continue with bel canto. Miss Horne's own husband wants her to become a Wagnerian soprano. She can do either and, for a time, both. He unique voice presents her with an embarrassment of riches. Whichever way she goes, she will be one of the most celebrated singers of her era.

Photo by Beth Bergman

Miss Sills as Maria Stuarda in Donizetti's opera.

III
Beverly Sills

With her husband, Peter Greenough, and their daughter, Muffy, in Milton, Massachusetts, shortly before they moved to New York.

M y third great diva is Beverly Sills, who, as I write this, has never sung at the Metropolitan Opera, but has remained faithfully as the prima donna of the New York City Opera. Miss Sills is a lyric coloratura, which means that her voice is much lighter than that of Joan Sutherland. She has sung most of the same repertory, however, and she makes up in brilliance what she lacks in weight. Not that her voice is in any way weak; it is just different in coloring and less heavy. She can fill the New York State Theatre with beautiful tone and without any special effort, and it might be noted that, because of inferior acoustics, the New York State Theatre is much harder to fill than the Metropolitan, which happens to have excellent acoustics. But the Beverly Sills voice has qualities of its own, which I shall do my best to analyze. Some vocal experts claim that she uses too much head voice and that consequently she hasn't quite the stability and assurance of singers like Joan Sutherland and Marilyn Horne. Maybe so, but I have never heard Miss Sills at a loss for assurance. Her fioritura is brought off with an easy agility that reminds one of splashing fountains, every drop glittering in the sun. The very lack of great weight in her voice permits her to toss off coloratura passages like a juggler tossing things easily into the air and retrieving them just as easily.

But the sure agility of Miss Sills' vocal fireworks is only a part of her total operatic personality. The quality of her voice is often touchingly childlike—something that, for all I know, may be connected with the overuse of head tones that theoreticians accuse her of. And this childlike quality is accompanied by an extraordinary range of vocal inflection. Miss Sills is, in my opinion, the greatest actress currently on the operatic stage; in fact, I would go further and say that she is a greater actress than even the fabled Maria Callas. The plangent quality of her voice and her enormous sensitivity to different emotions which is expressed in varying tones of voice are altogether extraordinary, and they are accompanied by enunciation of languages that is flawless. Often the subtle character of her voice reminds me of Claudia Muzio, who had this same expressive quality (as her recordings show). And unlike Muzio, Miss Sills is at home in French opera as well as Italian. Her French is superbly enunciated, so that every word, in an opera like *Manon,* can be understood by the audience, and her Italian enunciation is also very fine. Recently, she has brought an altogether unfamiliar sense of drama into the Elizabethan operas of Donizetti (*Maria Stuarda, Roberto Devereux,* and *Anna Bolena).* For generations these operas were considered showpieces for coloratura sopranos who merely stood and sang the notes accurately and with beautiful tone. Miss Sills has given them a new dimension, making them into dramas, as well as coloratura vehicles. She has even, from time to time, deliberately made her voice sound ugly in order to express fury or despair. All in order to add drama to her performance. Miss Sills is that rarity, an intellectual singer. She approaches her work with a thorough grasp of historical subject matter and a clear idea of exactly what she is going to do on the stage. She can move an audience to tears with no apparent effort at all, and bring it back to laughter in the same way.

When she made her debut at La Scala a few years ago, singing the difficult, pyrotechnical role of Pamira in Rossini's *The Siege of Corinth* with extraordinary success, her appearance was preceded by an incident of some significance. This occurred during the rehearsals of the opera. Miss Sills had been imported to do the role at the request of the conductor, Thomas Schippers, because the originally scheduled Pamira, Renata Scotto, was pregnant. As happens in the best of opera houses, Miss Scotto's costume was turned over to Miss Sills to wear. Now, Miss Scotto is a dark brunette, while Miss Sills is a flaming redhead. The costume was gold-colored—just right for Miss Scotto but an outlandish clash with Miss Sills' hair. Miss Sills requested that it be redone in silver. *"Sì, Signora,"* said the wardrobe mistress. But at the next rehearsal the same gold costume turned up. Miss Sills protested again. The wardrobe mistress was sympathetic and again promised to change it. Two more rehearsals, and the same costume continued to appear. Finally, when the gold costume was once again trotted out, this time in the view of the entire company, Miss Sills became exasperated. "Give me those scissors," she said to the wardrobe mistress, and thereupon cut the costume into three parts and handed them back. The chorus burst into applause. Someone they had taken for a good-natured American girl had turned out to be a real prima donna, complete with what Italians regard as the indispensable characteristic of temperament. Thenceforth, Miss Sills was regarded with awe backstage, as well as on the other side of the footlights. She was recognized as a true diva, and, needless to say, she got her silver costume. When the performance of *The Siege of Corinth* was over, she had become what in operatic circles is called a superstar. She immediately tripled her fees and started the superstar's formula—to her, quite uncongenial—of limiting her future engagements. No longer could Beverly Sills be expected to sing in places like Shreveport or Garden City. Only the world's greatest opera houses would be worthy of her, and they would want her in the roles for which she was most famous.

The display of temper during the rehearsal at La Scala was, of course, not the real source of her climb to superstardom. But, in a way, it symbolized the achievement. Anybody who can tell the wardrobe mistress of *any* leading opera house to go to hell must be somebody—somebody more, at any rate, than just a skillful American singer. And the fact that the episode took place at La

Scala, which Italians like to think of as the world's greatest temple of opera, added untold prestige. The peculiar glamor that attaches to a great diva is nowadays very much an Italian product. There was a time, long ago, when it was French, too. It is an old-fashioned thing, entailing the worship of a personality, as well as a voice, and Miss Sills had earned it. The fact that she is one of the greatest coloratura sopranos now extant was almost beside the question.

It is reasonable at this point to ask just what an operatic superstar is and how many of them exist. Well, a superstar is a singer who sings certain roles superlatively well (better than anyone else), who says no to most offers by smaller opera houses, who charges a fee of as much as ten thousand dollars per performance, and who is in the difficult position of having to reach a new peak every season, attaining new heights of skill and personal charm or dramatic force.

Always what has struck audiences most about Miss Sills has been her warmth of personality, her sense of drama, her charm, and her good looks, and these qualities have carried her through a career that has included most of the roles written for the lighter type of soprano, whether coloratura or simply lyric. (Indeed, at one point in her life she sang some dramatic-soprano roles, too, but such feats belong to the past.) On the stage, Miss Sills is a tall woman—too tall for some of the little-girl roles, like Sophie in *Der Rosenkavalier*. As she puts it, "Madame Butterfly I ain't." But by various subterfuges of bearing she manages, from time to time, to look smaller than she is. She has dark-brown eyes, a round, Slavic face, a ski-jump nose, full lips, and natural high coloring, and she smiles easily. Most important of all, perhaps, she has an extraordinarily slim waist—an enormous visual advantage for an opera singer. Put together, all these qualities, plus her red hair, make her look a little like a doll on a Christmas tree. In short, by operatic standards Miss Sills is a beauty. Not since the time of Geraldine Farrar, in all probability, has the operatic stage witnessed her particular combination of femininity, good looks, and spectacular vocal accomplishments.

Miss Sills suddenly became a star (not yet a superstar) in 1966, when she first sang Cleopatra in that New York City Opera production of Handel's *Giulio Cesare* at the New York State Theatre. Audiences and critics realized for the first time that they were in the presence of a diva of historical importance. She tossed off all of Handel's difficult fioritura with exemplary intonation, faultless agility, and a warmth of tone that is seldom encountered in singers of her type. Scales, arpeggios, and complicated ornamentations emerged from her throat with the natural ease of a summer shower of rain. And, beyond this, there was an expressive elasticity to her singing that made every mood, and every dramatic change of mood, evident to her audience. The production was a stunning one. Cesare was sung by the great, modest, and generally underrated bass Norman Treigle, while Julius Rudel, the company's artistic director, conducted in the pit. The evening as a whole was a triumph—a more brilliant occasion than anything that had recently happened at the Metropolitan Opera. There was an ebullient realization on everybody's part that New York's own opera company and New York's own singers had reached a peak of success that—for the time being, at least—left the big, international Metropolitan Opera behind. And the largest factor in the triumph was Miss Sills—charmingly seducing the Roman Emperor, singing like a nightingale, projecting across the footlights the most attractive of operatic personalities.

Some in the audience were surprised. Others were not. The faithful public of the New York City Opera had been watching and listening to Miss Sills for a little more than a decade, witnessing her rise from what is called a "utility singer"—that is to say, a useful minor artist who can be put into various roles at short notice—to a singer of leading roles. On October 29, 1955, she made her first appearance with the company in the dramatically rewarding but not vocally taxing role of Rosalinda in *Die Fledermaus,* for which she had been hired by Joseph Rosenstock, then the company's general director. That fall, she also substituted for Jean Fenn in Tchaikovsky's *The Golden Slippers.* A year later

Rosenstock left the company, and his successor, Erich Leinsdorf, cast her in the role of Philine in *Mignon*. Here, for the first time, her coloratura technique had a chance to display itself—as it continued to do in the role of Violetta in *La Traviata,* under Julius Rudel, who succeeded Leinsdorf in 1957. (The Italian conductor Arturo Basile, who made his debut here conducting her *Traviata,* said of her, "In all Italy, there is not a singer who can do a comparable Violetta.") For several years, she was most familiar to audiences as the heroine of Douglas Moore's *The Ballad of Baby Doe,* and her attractive appearance and her shrewd sense of drama—along with the fine acting and singing ability of Walter Cassel, who did the role of the Colorado mining king Horace Tabor—helped make this into perhaps the most successful American opera ever written. But Miss Sills was still a utility singer, and the company still inhabited the old, dingy City Center of Music and Art, a former Shriners' temple, on Fifty-fifth Street. Then, in 1963, came a turning point—Donna Anna to Norman Treigle's Don Giovanni, a showy coloratura role calling for considerable dramatic ability. The following year, she sang Marguérite in *Faust.* The year after that, she did all four soprano roles in *Tales of Hoffmann,* and her effortless agility as the singing doll Olympia confirmed her position as the reigning queen of the New York City Opera and, with Treigle's magnificent bass, one of its two principal attractions. But her career had matured very slowly. She was already in her middle thirties.

Many people have remarked, sometimes with puzzlement, on the slowness with which Miss Sills came to superstardom. Partly, it was because of family troubles, but the big reason, in the opinion of most informed operagoers, was the situation of the New York City Opera. Opera is to some extent an exercise in glamor, as well as in vocalism. The prima donna of New York's second-ranking opera company—a popular-priced one that played in the City Center—could hardly hope to rival the divas of the lavishly supported and expensive Metropolitan, even though she sang as well as, or better than, they did. A few critics were proclaiming Miss

Sills' virtues, but the general public, paying low box-office prices to sit in an ugly auditorium, continued to think of the New York City Opera as a second-class company. In 1966, however, all this suddenly changed. The New York City Opera moved to the New York State Theatre, which, though not acoustically perfect, was by far the most attractive of all the theaters in the newly built Lincoln Center for the Performing Arts. Standing at one side of the new Metropolitan Opera House, it was equally glamorous and even more elegant. With the help of Ford Foundation money, the company rebuilt its sets on more lavish lines. Though still performing at popular prices and playing a shorter season than the Metropolitan, it began—through ingenuity rather than financial outlay—to rival the bigger one. Under these circumstances, the New York City Opera's singers began to seem as glamorous as those of the Met, and Miss Sills, the company's faithful prima donna, was for the first time seen and heard in the appropriate setting. Rudolf Bing, director of the Metropolitan, who has been known to lure away a rival company's best singers, made several offers to Miss Sills following her triumph in *Giulio Cesare*, which was one of the first new productions in the new house. But Miss Sills has remained true to the company with which she grew to stardom. "It's a lot better to be the top diva of a smaller company than to be one of several at the Met," she has said. "Besides, it would be silly for me to be singing, say, *Lucia* across the plaza the same week I might be doing it at the State Theatre. Someday, of course, I'd like to sing at the Metropolitan, but I think I'll wait awhile. The New York City Opera is my home company, and it always will be. I'll sing there as long as they want me."

After the triumph in *Giulio Cesare* Miss Sills sang Constanze in *The Abduction from the Seraglio,* the Queen of the Night in *The Magic Flute,* and the Queen of Shemakha in *Le Coq d'Or.* Then she embarked on two roles in French opera, for which she received critical acclaim—Manon, and a restudied Marguérite in a brand-new production of *Faust.* The Manon was the finest seen by New Yorkers in many decades, and her audiences practically wept with her. "You know, Sarah Bernhardt was a redhead, too," a critic said after one performance—a remark that may or may not have been irrelevant. One of the factors in Miss Sills' striking impersonations of both Manon and Marguérite was her flawless French diction. The scarcity of fine French singers, and the common practice at the Metropolitan of replacing them with Italians, had made elegant French a rarity on the New York operatic stage. Miss Sills' enunciation added a subtle aura to these roles and gave them an authenticity that was new to many of her listeners. Meanwhile, she continued her brilliant coloratura repertoire with *Lucia,* to which she brought an entirely new and quite individual conception. Her Lucia was no operatic doll tossing off vocal fireworks but a thoroughly thought-out character—feminine, vulnerable, heartbreaking—and her Mad Scene was a remarkable tour de force of acting. Vocally, Miss Sills was as brilliant as one could wish—more brilliant than anyone can expect today, except, perhaps, in the case of the heavier but no less accurate Lucia of Joan Sutherland. But it was more than a vocal exhibition. Miss Sills seemed to be the archetype of beauty betrayed, and her audience was in love with her. Her next role was that of Queen Elizabeth in Donizetti's *Roberto Devereux*—a difficult coloratura vehicle and a part that can be made into a tremendous stage spectacle by a great actress. She went on to sing *Anna Bolena* the following year, and then *Maria Stuarda,* completing the Donizetti Elizabethan trilogy.

The thoroughness with which Miss Sills learns her roles is remarkable. She is an excellent pianist, and studies them all at the keyboard. By the time she is finished, she knows not only her own role in the opera, but all the other roles, too. "There are one or two exceptions," she said the other day. "I don't know the last scene of *Lucia,* for instance, but that's because I don't sing a note in it. Generally, I can sing every role in every act of every opera I know." Moreover, before she undertakes a new role, Miss Sills exhausts the literature about it. If it represents a historical character, her research may be very extensive. "First, I eat up the libretto and work out all its possible meanings," she said. "If an Italian word, for example, has a slightly different implication from its dictionary definition, I find it. This happens quite a lot in librettos." Then she reads everything she can dig up about the character. A reporter who called on her in her New York apartment before the opening of *Roberto Devereux* found her studying up on Queen Elizabeth from an assortment of about thirty books, some of them biographies of Elizabeth, others historical studies of her times. "I've just about got that woman cold," she said happily, and added, "I don't want to be an exhibitionistic coloratura who merely sings notes. I'm interested in the *character*." After she has absorbed all the available historical and biographical data, she starts going over the music at the piano—and, of course, her knowledge of the piano score tells her what to expect from the orchestra later. Then she calls on her coach, Roland Gagnon, who is otherwise occupied as a voice teacher in the drama division of the Juilliard School and as an occasional conductor. He will have prepared a number of embellishments—those little turns, extra scales, arpeggios, trills, and so on, in eighteenth-century and early-nineteenth-century bel-canto opera, which every knowledgeable coloratura performs in her own way—for her to choose from. She feels that these embellishments are dictated not only by the style of the composer but also by the character she is interpreting. "I always decide on them after I have come to a conclusion about the character," she said. "I never use embellishments that don't seem to fit the character. All my embellishments in *Lucia*, for example, are done for dramatic purposes. For Queen Elizabeth, I went slow on embellishments. After all, you can't add too many embellishments to the Queen of England."

With the embellishments decided upon, Mr. Gagnon then takes her through a period of intensive coaching. Even Miss Sills, though she is a thorough musician (a rarity among opera singers), needs a coach—to help polish phrasing and the accents of the language, and, above all, to provide a second party to listen carefully to what she has learned by herself. After this, she is ready for rehearsals and performances. "Everything I put into opera is instinct," she has said. But it is quite obvious that this "instinct" is accompanied by a great deal of plain intelligence and horse sense.

At home, as a private person, Miss Sills seems anything but the sedulous scholar she actually is. Her manner is ebullient, hearty, and altogether illustrative of the nickname Bubbles, which has followed her throughout her life. It is impossible to call her Miss Sills after more than half an hour of acquaintance. Even to comparative strangers, she inevitably becomes Beverly, if not quite Bubbles. The warmth and femininity that she shows on the stage are part of her real personality. She is irrepressibly talkative— about opera, about people, even about her most intimate joys and sorrows. She is a compulsive letter writer, who answers all her enormous fan mail, even if it is only with an autographed photograph. To her closer friends, who include her press agents, Edgar Vincent and Marjorie Samuel, she writes exuberantly while on tour, delighted with every moment of her life as a great diva. From Manila she once wrote Miss Samuel this quasi-poetic note:

> I'm a queen
> I'm a queen
> I'm a goddam queen
> I swear to God
> 4 body guards (it's a big body) and presents and presidential suites and chauffeurs and limousines and banquets and parties and maids and secretaries and hairdressers.
> Goodbye forever, it is all too much
>
> Yours,
> Beverly

Friends say that if you are depressed, talking to her is like champagne. She enjoys singing and often makes her audience aware of her enjoyment, especially in comedy roles. She would probably sing whether she was paid to or not. Like most singers, she has a number of superstitions. One is about a pair of shoes that an MIT physicist once gave her which she believes make her magically impervious to both sea- and airsickness. The secret is contained in a metal strip down the inside of the sole, and she is very serious about its efficacy, wearing these shoes whenever she flies—which is, of course, quite often. Another of these odd notions is her insistence that her mother, Mrs. Shirley Silverman, escaped from Russia in a pickle barrel. Since her mother left Russia by way of the Trans-Siberian Railroad to Vladivostok, and eventually sailed to the United States from Yokohama aboard the Japanese freighter *Panama Maru,* the question arises just how long she stayed in that pickle barrel. Mrs. Silverman herself, who looks like an older version of Beverly, says that the only possible connection between this fantasy and the truth is that as a child during a pogrom she and her grandmother were once hidden in pickle barrels by her grandfather as some Cossacks were riding by their house, near Odessa. Her trip via the Trans-Siberian Railroad was a normal one, taken in 1917 at the urging of her father, an inventor and engineer who had emigrated to the United States and taken a job in Brooklyn with the United States government. He had shrewdly seen the approach of the Russian Revolution; in fact, his daughter left Russia in the very week that Kerensky came to power. In Brooklyn, Shirley met and married a Rumanian-born insurance man named Morris Silverman; they moved to Detroit, where Morris joined his brother's construction business, and after a few years they returned to Brooklyn. There Beverly Sills, née Belle Silverman, was born in 1929.

Shirley Silverman was interested in music, and she used to visit the secondhand-record shops on Fourteenth Street to buy recordings of her favorite singers, one of whom was Amelita Galli-Curci. "I used to play them while I was doing my housework," she said recently. "I was a great opera fan; I used to go to the Metropolitan quite often." Her daughter began imitating Galli-Curci's records in her small, childish voice, and by the time she was seven she knew twenty-three arias by heart and could sing all the fioritura, though she had learned the words purely by mimicry and hadn't the slightest idea what they meant. She was sent to dancing school and to P.S. 91, in Brooklyn, and later to Winthrop Junior High, where she was considered a bright pupil. Practically from infancy, she was involved in show business, first on a weekly radio program on WOR called *Rainbow House with Big Brother Bob Emery,* where she was known as Bubbles Silverman. Already she was a trouper. She didn't miss a program for four years—not even when she had the mumps and quickly emptied the studio. At the age of nine, and with the new name of Beverly Sills, she was singing all those coloratura arias on Major Bowes' Capitol *Family* program, including "Caro nome" and the "Bell Song" from *Lakmé.* "I was born into the age of Shirley Temple," she said the other day. "Child prodigies were all over the place. Then I graduated into the Deanna Durbin era of teen-age stars like Bobby Breen, Gloria Jean, and Ann Blyth." Major Bowes became ill in 1941, and she was shifted to the *Cresta Blanca Carnival,* where one of her co-stars was Robert Merrill, the Metropolitan baritone. Shortly before that, at the age of ten, she had played Elaine Raleigh in the soap opera *Our Gal Sunday,* a part that lasted thirty-six weeks and involved a little girl whose singing in the forest was so engaging that a famous prima donna eventually adopted her and took her to Europe—with the result that Beverly was written out of the script. By this time, she was making sixty-seven dollars and fifty cents per performance, and this was supplemented when she did the ubiquitous radio commercial "Rinso White, Rinso Bright, happy little washday song."

But Beverly's mother was, and still is, a woman of much common sense, and she knew that this kid stuff would not last forever. Besides, she wanted Beverly to aim at more serious things, and she had already taken steps in that direction. In 1936, Mrs. Silverman had seen a picture of the late Estelle Liebling, Galli-Curci's coach, on the cover of the *Musical Courier* with the caption "Teacher of Operatic, Stage, Screen, and Radio Artists" (Miss Liebling's brother edited the magazine), and she took Beverly to Miss Liebling's studio, on West Fifty-fifth Street, for an audition. There was some confusion at the outset. Miss Liebling thought that it was

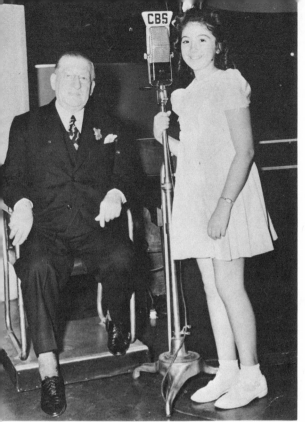

Miss Sills as a child with the late Major Bowes on a CBS broadcast.

Miss Sills with her teacher, Miss Estelle Liebling.

As Cleopatra in Handel's *Giulio Cesare* presented by the New York City Opera.

Miss Sills as Queen Elizabeth in Donizetti's *Roberto Devereux*.

Left: Miss Sills as Lucia in Donizetti's *Lucia di Lammermoor* at the start of the Mad Scene.

Mrs. Silverman who wanted the audition. "Leave the little girl outside," she said rather peremptorily. "But I wanted your advice about what to do with her," said Mrs. Silverman. "Put her in kindergarten," suggested Miss Liebling. Then Mrs. Silverman patiently explained that it was her seven-year-old daughter who wanted the audition. Now, the training of coloratura sopranos at the age of seven is almost unheard of. Most of them start after adolescence. Miss Liebling was extremely skeptical, but when she heard Bubbles Silverman sing, she was astonished and agreed to take her on as a pupil. Miss Liebling gave her a fifteen-minute lesson each Saturday and insisted that she also practice scales with a pitch pipe for ten minutes every day at home (she was allowed to go only up to B, even though she could sing G) and that she study French and Italian—one or the other every day—with a couple of maiden ladies who lived upstairs. Meanwhile, Beverly was studying piano with Paolo Gallico, father of Paul Gallico, the novelist. The Silvermans had by this time moved to Sea Gate, and Beverly had a long subway ride to Miss Liebling's studio. Her various lessons plus her radio engagements took up a great deal of her time. The regimen was a tough one. But Miss Liebling took more than an ordinary interest in her pupil. "She taught me manners, for one thing, and she taught me discipline, too," Beverly recalls today. "She had a rug in her studio that had a gold-colored spot in the middle of it. I had to stand on that spot while I was singing, and not move from it. For a seven-year-old, that was pretty difficult." From the age of thirteen, Beverly studied operatic stagecraft with the late Désiré Defrère, an experienced old opera director who had worked with practically every opera company from San Francisco to the Metropolitan. "I learned fifty operatic roles," she remembers. "Miss Liebling simply poured them into me." Defrère was nonplussed. "You just wind her up and she sings," he noted with surprise.

Beverly was undergoing a period of apprenticeship. She sang everywhere that people wanted her. Miss Liebling thought that auditions were valuable experiences whether you won or lost, and, as Mrs. Silverman has noted, Beverly never felt that she had to win anything at all costs. She was a graceful loser. But the Silverman family finances were a little cramped. Beverly had two older brothers, one of whom was being put through medical school, and expenses were high. At seventeen, she won three hundred dollars on Arthur Godfrey's "Talent Scouts," and sang at the Waldorf-Astoria for ladies' luncheons at five dollars a performance. At nineteen, she was singing and playing the piano until two in the morning in a nightclub on the upper East Side for tips, the politest of which arrived enclosed in envelopes. Then she would get up at eight o'clock for her lesson with Miss Liebling. In 1945, when she was sixteen and had graduated from school, she auditioned for J. J. Shubert and was signed to a contract as the "youngest prima donna in captivity," to sing Gilbert and Sullivan's *Countess Maritia, The Merry Widow,* and *Rose Marie* on the road. She had her first high heels and upswept hairdo for the performances. Her father, Morris, was dead set against all this early participation in the sometimes sordid field of show business. He claimed that Mrs. Silverman was bringing up their daughter to be a "singing showgirl," and for a time he refused even to speak to Beverly. But the practical stage experience she was getting was invaluable. In February, 1947, when she was still seventeen, she sang in grand opera for the first time, as Frasquita in *Carmen* with the Philadelphia Civic Grand Opera Company. In 1950, she began two seasons of coast-to-coast tours as a member of the Charles Wagner Opera Company, riding in a bus from small town to small town and doing the role of Micaela in *Carmen* sixty-three times in sixty-three successive one-night stands. Earlier, in New York, she had been offered a scholarship at what was then Fairleigh Dickinson Junior College, because she was particularly good in math. But she never accepted it. Her grueling life in show business and tank-town opera seemed to point in the direction that she and her mother thought she should go.

Every year, from 1951 onward, Beverly auditioned for the New York City Opera, then under Joseph Rosenstock. She was always unsuccessful; Rosenstock thought that she was a good singer but that she didn't have any personality. Julius Rudel, who was the piano accompanist for these auditions, has pointed out that Beverly was not a good audition singer. "The dumb singers with nothing between their ears usually do well at auditions," he said. "A singer with brains often fails, just because he is only too aware of his surroundings." After four years of unsuccessful auditions singing things like "Caro nome" and 'Una voce poco fa," Beverly got herself a couple of blood-and-thunder arias to sing for Rosenstock. They were excerpts from *Tosca* and *Andrea Chénier*—both dramatic-soprano arias totally unsuited to her voice. Rosenstock then agreed that she had some personality, and the role in *Die Fledermaus* resulted.

But *Die Fledermaus* was not Miss Sills' debut in big-time opera. Two years previously, Gaetano Merola, the impresario of the San Francisco Opera, had come to New York looking for singers, and Beverly had auditioned for him. He signed her immediately to do Donna Elvira in *Don Giovanni*, Elena in *Mefistofele,* and some minor roles, at a fee of a hundred and seventy-five dollars a week, and, in addition, invited her to stay with his family in San Francisco. The San Francisco Opera was, and still is, one of the few American opera houses with Metropolitan standards, and Beverly was thrilled at the opportunity, especially of singing Donna Elvira (she had never even heard *Don Giovanni*)—a difficult role that is usually done by much more mature singers. She arrived in San Francisco with only ten dollars in her purse. Merola did not meet her at the airport, as he had promised to do. She felt lost, but she looked up his address in the telephone book and began making her way there by various buses and streetcars. It took her four hours, and when she arrived she discovered that Merola had died the previous day. However, she was able to get a room in the Whitcomb Hotel, a hangout for show people ("I cooked frankfurters on the radiator," she has said of it), and Kurt Adler, the company's chorus master, quickly stepped into Merola's shoes as head of the San Francisco Opera—a position he still holds.

Beverly sang the roles that were planned for her, and while there is no record that she stood San Francisco on its ear, she was successful enough to go on to Portland, where she sang Violetta in *La Traviata* opposite the then already famous Jan Peerce. Her father probably would have approved of her operatic career. But he had died when she was twenty and still working for the Shuberts. Earlier, they had become reconciled, and at his death Beverly was so overcome with grief that she did not sing for several months. Only the persistent persuasion of Miss Liebling led her to resume singing.

In 1955, during her first season with the New York City Opera, the company went on tour, winding up in Cleveland, where she sang Rosalinda in *Die Fledermaus*. A party was held for the company at the Cleveland Press Club, and though Beverly was reluctant to attend, Rudel insisted that she do so. The president of the Press Club was Peter Greenough, a financial columnist and part owner of the Cleveland *Plain Dealer*. Greenough was a wealthy man and a descendant of a long line of New Englanders that actually reached back to John Alden. He was also an Air Force hero, most of whose squadron had been shot down during the Sicilian campaign in the Second World War. He invited Beverly to go to a Chinese restaurant for dinner. She couldn't accept, because she was to sing that night, but she invited *him* to a party after the performance. The tour was over, and ordinarily Beverly would have rushed home to Mother in New York. But she stayed on for a couple of days, during which Greenough showed up with two of his three children and asked her to marry him. Back in New York, Beverly told her mother, "I met a man I think I could marry." Her mother was overjoyed; Beverly was twenty-six. "But he's married and has three children." Her mother burst into tears. Actually, Greenough and his wife had separated, and in the subsequent divorce he got custody of the children. He and Beverly were married—on the gold spot on Estelle Liebling's rug—and she, not content to be merely a stepmother, formally adopted Peter's children. For a year or two, they lived in Cleveland and Beverly

95

held her career in abeyance, coming to New York only occasionally to see her mother and Miss Liebling, and to sing a few performances at the New York City Opera. Sometimes she would simply take a plane from Cleveland, meet her mother at the airport, have a short conversation, and take another plane back. Meanwhile, Rudel, upset at losing most of the services of his most promising soprano, wrote to her constantly, suggesting new roles. (He always addressed her as "Dear Bubbeleh.") But Beverly seemed perfectly content to be a housewife and mother. She bore Peter two children—a little girl, referred to as Muffy, in 1959, and a boy, known as Bucky, in 1961. By the time Bucky was born, the Greenoughs had moved to Boston, where Peter worked as a columnist for the *Globe*. Not long afterward, Beverly made a discovery that was to be the principal tragedy of her life; Muffy was totally deaf, and Bucky was retarded. "I do my weeping alone," she said but the discovery was heartbreaking. The children were sent to appropriate schools. Bucky is still in the Dr. Franklin Perkins School in Lancaster, Massachusetts. Muffy went to the Boston School for the Deaf to learn lipreading and how to talk. For a long time, words like "papa," "mama," and "baby" looked exactly alike to her, but nowadays she can detect nasal and guttural sounds almost uncannily and can talk quite fluently, although it takes a little time to get used to her manner of speaking. She will probably never hear her mother sing, but she is actually quite a brilliant little girl and has attended many of her mother's performances. She can act out all the roles in *Tales of Hoffmann*— not only her mother's but those of all the other characters as well. Her ambition at the moment is to be a veterinarian.

Looking back on it all, Beverly says "In a way, retarded children are satisfying. Everything is a triumph. Even getting Bucky to manage to get a spoon to his mouth was a triumph. God compensates." But the blow was one of those deep wounds that are apt to change one's life. "I would willingly give up my whole career if I could have just one normal child," she has said. But Beverly is what she calls "an optimistic fatalist." She resumed singing as a kind of therapy. The tragedy had given her a new self-assurance. Having tasted the worst, she no longer had the slightest doubt of her ability to weather the ups and downs of her career. Not only was there an added degree of self-assurance; there was a new emotional depth to her operatic characterizations—a new tenderness, a new willingness to communicate her personal sorrows to audiences, even though she was doing it indirectly, by way of a tragic character. It was at this time, in fact, that the mature diva Beverly Sills began to make a profound impression on critics and on the public.

Today, the Greenoughs live in New York, in a conventional but large apartment on Central Park West. Peter is a big, burly man who doesn't at all mind being a prima donna's husband. In fact, he attends most of her performances. At Beverly's suggestion, however, they have made a strict financial arrangement. The fees that Beverly receives are her own, and go into furthering her career. Eventually, they will go into a trust fund for Muffy, which she will receive on her twentieth birthday. Peter's fortune supports the family. None of his money is spent in any way on Beverly's professional activities. "After all, I wouldn't want people to say that my husband's money was being spent to further my ambitions, and I want the satisfaction of making a career on my own," Beverly says. "I didn't want the fun of it to be taken away from me." The apartment is inhabited by Peter, Beverly, Muffy, and a ferociously affectionate little white poodle named Gigi. Central Park, opposite, offers a place to walk. The Greenoughs have an Irish housekeeper (who is also Beverly's hairdresser) named Oona, to whom Muffy is devoted. Nevertheless, Beverly is much concerned about being with her daughter and has canceled many foreign engagements, or parts of them, so that she can remain at home. Her recent raising of her fees was partly motivated by this need to stay with Muffy. If people want to pay her high prices, she will go; if they think that she's too expensive, that's all right, too—she will have just that much more time with Muffy. In the summer, when she and Peter are not traveling (he accompanies her on practically all her foreign engagements), the Greenoughs go to West Chop, on Martha's Vineyard, where they live in a large house that has been owned by his family for more than a hundred years. There they go boating (Beverly always in her special seasickness-proof shoes), and Peter plays tennis, in spite of a bad knee that he got playing football at Harvard. Both Beverly and Peter frequently take to dieting, since both are inclined to overweight, and they are often observed by friends sadly dining on a hard-boiled egg apiece and a little cottage cheese. They seldom go out socially, and they hate cocktail parties, though they occasionally have a couple of guests in for dinner. "We are very private people," Miss Sills observes.

The Greenoughs, at home in their Manhattan apartment, seem to be a very happy family. Muffy talks away as if talking were an exotic discovery. But nobody talks more than Beverly. "God forbid I should be quiet!" she exclaims in mock Brooklynese. "I even talk when we are playing bridge. Peter can't stand that, and he's right—you shouldn't talk during a bridge game." She went on to describe something that had happened during a performance of *Tales of Hoffmann* in McAllen, Texas. Norman Treigle, who was doing the role of the sinister Dr. Miracle, dropped the medicine bottles on the floor of the stage. Beverly walked on the broken glass in her bare feet and cut herself badly. A doctor suggested a tetanus shot. "What would happen if I did get tetanus?" "Well, for one thing," the doctor replied, "You wouldn't be able to talk." "That did it!" Beverly recalled. "The idea of not being able to talk! Why, talking is the way I warm up my voice!"

Besides playing bridge, at which Peter admits she is very good (he taught her), Beverly is, and has always been, a good poker player. On a bus trip during one tour, she told a reporter recently, she completely cleaned out the tenor John Alexander. She added that she also likes to do Double-Crostics and difficult crossword puzzles. At this point, Gigi rushed like a cannonball into the interviewer's lap. "Dumb," Beverly commented while shooing her off. "All the dumb dogs come to the Greenoughs. We've had a succession of dumb dogs." Then she went on, as if there had been no change of subject, "When I made my debut with the New York City Opera, in 1955, it was a repertory company. That meant that everybody had to do everything—sometimes roles that were not appropriate at all. We *had* to act, because our roles were so often unsuited to our voices. But that was part of the job. When you're a utility singer, you don't have much choice. You sing everything they ask you to. Now it's altogether different. They pick the opera to go with my voice." But, superstar or not, Beverly sings at the New York City Opera for a twelfth of the fees she receives elsewhere.

Miss Sills' older brothers are both highly successful. Stanley Sills is an executive with IT & T, specializing in publishing, and Sidney Silverman is a prominent obstetrician on Long Island. "Somebody remarked a while ago that my obstetrician brother doesn't attend many of my performances," she once observed. "Why should he? I don't attend his deliveries." Though there is a warm relationship today between Beverly and her brothers, there is, as one might guess, a very special relationship between Beverly and her mother. Mrs. Silverman has the same warmth of personality that characterizes Beverly. She is a very motherly woman, representing a strong maternal tradition, which Beverly has inherited. She is proud that none of her children left her until they got married. Mrs. Silverman now lives in a small apartment on Central Park South, where she keeps Beverly's old baby-grand piano. She is an accomplished seamstress—who used to make all of her daughter's concert gowns—and a talented amateur painter.

Probably few people who have seen Miss Sills in roles of betrayed innocence—Manon in the first act, or Lucia—realize that behind that guileless feminine façade, and under that red hair, there lies a brain that works like a machine. During the rehearsals for *The Siege of Corinth* at La Scala, she and Marilyn Horne discovered that the stage designer had put a scrim between them and the audience. All singers hate scrim, because they think it muffles their voices. "Well, how are we going to get rid of that scrim?" asked Miss Horne. "I'll manage it," said Miss Sills. Nothing much happened for a while, and Miss Horne got impatient. "Don't worry," said Miss Sills. Then she purposely made an error in her part, and the conductor, Thomas Schippers, took her to task for it. "Well," said Miss Sills airily, "if you are willing to follow me through the whole scene, it will come out all right, but the fact is I can't see you conduct through that scrim." No conductor is going to relinquish his control over tempos, and so the scrim was quickly removed. "You see," said Miss Sills to Miss Horne, "it's simple to get your way." This sort of roundabout approach to problems has been typical of Beverly since childhood, and she has pretty nearly always got her way—with conductors, with fellow artists, and with managers. Actually, her manager, Ludwig Lustig, is not the most prominent in his profession, but he is notably faithful to his clients, and he does more for her than any big management corporation would do. "He always shows up at my performances to say 'Toy, toy, toy!'" Miss Sills says. "That's a polite remnant of the custom of spitting three times on an artist for good luck just before he goes onstage." Similarly, in looking for a recording company Miss Sills chose Westminster, because it was a comparatively small outfit. (As a result of mergers, she now appears on the ABC Audio Treasury Series.) Her connection with the company has been mutually rewarding; her first solo album was a best seller for two years, and at one time she had three albums among the top fifteen. When she is recording, she is smart enough to sing differently from the way she does in the opera house. For example, when she pushes Enrico away during the Mad Scene in *Lucia,* she puts a hysterical inflection—almost a scream—into her voice for dramatic effect. In the recording studio, however, she does not scream at this point but merely sings the high note that is indicated in a nice tone of voice; without the visual drama, there is not much sense in making ugly sounds for the sake of the dramatic situation. It is a remarkable fact that when Miss Sills does things in an unorthodox way, audiences, after some criticism, begin to like them, and to consider them part of the Beverly Sills personality. For a long time, directors, publicity people, and coaches didn't like the way she took a bow. She merely bobbed her head and smiled. "We've got to get her to bow better," one of them argued. But Beverly went on bowing the same way, and finally audiences accepted her bow as part of her individual charm. There has also been some criticism of the costumes she wears for concert appearances. She runs to bright blues, which some people consider a bit garish. Most singers wear black or dark blue to concerts. But last year, when Beverly appeared at the benefit concert honoring Pablo Casals in Philharmonic Hall—she is a great admirer of Casals, and she had flown from the Coast to take part in the event, flying back immediately when it was over—she turned up in the brightest of light-blue gowns. Eleanor Lambert, the oracle of the fashion world, who was present, remarked later, "Beverly Sills has a very good idea of her body. She doesn't try to hide the fact that she's a large woman. She looks statuesque. She plays up her good points, like her complexion, her neckline, and so forth. She has a natural kind of elegance." Like Nellie Melba, three generations before her, Beverly is a style setter and an individualist. Perhaps peaches and toast will someday be named for her, too.

Ever since she was a little girl, Miss Sills has gone to the opera to hear other people sing, and she continues to do so today. Her favorite singer (until her retirement) was Maria Callas. What she admired about Mademoiselle Callas, besides her coloratura technique, was her stunning dramatic skill and her ability to color every phrase with meaning. These are qualities that Miss Sills herself has acquired, though she is visually an entirely different type from the dark, aquiline Mademoiselle Callas. She is very outspoken in her opinions about singers, casting, and the running of opera houses, and her experience gives her the right to criticize. For a long time, she and her husband have been on the board of directors of the Opera Company of Boston, where they have coped with the whims of the woman who is undoubtedly the greatest, and also the most spendthrift, opera director in America, Sarah Caldwell. "I know a lot about the administrative side of opera," Miss Sills once remarked. "I've earned my living as a singer for more than half my life, and I know about the cost of costumes, about contracts, about union negotiations, about bargaining. That kind of job I could handle very well. Someday, when I can no longer sing, I'd like to run my own opera company. Directing doesn't interest me, but administration does." It follows that she has strong opinions about administrators. Of Mr. Bing, the recently retired general manager of the Metropolitan, she once remarked, "I don't think he likes bel-canto opera. After all, what has he let Joan Sutherland sing? *Sonnambula,* which is a silly opera. *Lucia, Norma.* That's about it. And his casting in French opera was ridiculous. It is stupid to cast Corelli as Werther when Gedda was around. I can't lie. I've been around too many years—and when I say I'm in my forties I think I'm talking about somebody else anyhow."

Like every intelligent singer, Miss Sills is aware that her voice is not going to last forever. There are some roles that she would like to sing while she is still in top form, among them Medea and Norma. For later on, she has planned some roles that are less exigent of agility and high notes—the Marschallin in *Der Rosenkavalier,* Desdemona, and some others. But at the moment her big problem is to cut down on her appearances and say no to offers of engagements. Her career as a superstar is so recent that she finds herself cluttered with previous commitments. In 1971 she sang *Lucia* at Covent Garden and *Traviata* in Berlin, and gave a concert at the Salle Pleyel, in Paris. Later, she sang at the San Francisco Opera for the first time since 1953, opening the season as Manon. She also sang with the Opera Company of Boston; in Bloomington, Illinois; with the Los Angeles Philharmonic; in Jacksonville, Florida; and in almost twenty other cities—plus filling her regular engagements with the New York City Opera. Altogether, she makes about sixty operatic appearances a year, and this, she thinks, is too many. One trouble is that she likes to sing and can hardly bear to turn down an engagement. "I would like to sing every role ever written for the soprano voice," she admits. But circumstances now dictate a more Spartan attitude. So far, in deciding which engagements to accept and which to reject she has adopted the principle "What would Birgit Nilsson say?" and has acted accordingly. This, of course, is merely a prop until she gets used to her role of superstar. Ultimately, Beverly Sills will make up her own mind.

Behind the public aspect of her career, Miss Sills is very concerned about being a good mother. Some time ago she canceled *Anna Bolena* from her schedule at the Teatro Colón, in Buenos Aires, and sang only *Manon*. This cut her engagement from six weeks to three, and it was done so that she could get home to Muffy. "Muffy was having term-end ceremonies," she explained, "and she would have been the only girl there without a mother." The last time Miss Sills went to Europe, she came home to find Muffy biting her nails and showing other signs of feeling rejected. "I know how important La Scala is, but here is where I hang my voice," she remarked. "The only thing I enjoy in Europe is the actual performance. I don't particularly enjoy travel. And I don't particularly like the atmosphere in Italian opera houses, where the Italians just can't imagine great singers' coming from anywhere else, and think they are freaks if they do. Actually, the finest voices and the most intelligent singers today come from America, not Italy. Take Norman Treigle, for instance. He's like a brother to me. He is very modest. He lives only for his moments onstage. He is one of the great unappreciated artists of our time." One gets the impression that Miss Sills doesn't care whether she sings in Europe or not. She would be perfectly content to be the reigning prima donna of the New York City Opera, as well as a wife and mother.

One day, Julius Rudel's wife, Rita, walked into Miss Sills' dressing room, where a throng of fans were asking for autographs or merely getting a glimpse of the diva. Both Mrs. Rudel and Miss Sills have round, Slavic faces, and people often think they are related. "This must be your sister," somebody in the crowd said to Miss Sills. "Yes, indeed," Miss Sills replied. "And I'll tell you a secret. She's not only my sister—she's married to Mr. Rudel. That's how I got so far in this company. You have to have pull."

As Princess Turandot in Puccini's *Turandot*.

IV
Birgit Nilsson

Miss Nilsson on her father's farm in Sweden.   *Photograph by Anders Svahn*

For a period of about two and a half months every year, a sturdily built black-haired Swedish soprano named Birgit Nilsson regularly emerges from the Hotel Alden, on upper Central Park West, puts two fingers in her mouth, whistles for a taxi with a shrillness that would do credit to a longshoreman, and makes her way to the Metropolitan Opera. Once there, she does her singing in a businesslike manner, throwing her huge voice across the footlights, acting with great intelligence, and generally making a remarkable impression on those who hear her. When she has finished singing, she exits into the wings (often complaining to the nearest stagehand that her feet hurt) and assumes the prosaic demeanor of a busy housewife. She goes to her dressing room, where, if it is an intermission, she sucks on an orange. If it is the end of the opera, an attendant brings her a jigger of aquavit, a glass of beer, and a herring—a very special sort of Swedish herring, from a hoard that she brings over with her regularly from Europe. Miss Nilsson doesn't care for champagne, the traditional drink of famous divas. She doesn't even particularly care for the crowd of admirers and autograph seekers who are apt to throng an opera star's dressing room after a performance. "I don't like that expression 'prima donna,'" she once said. "I feel more like a working soprano."

Miss Nilsson is unquestionably the most admired luminary of the Wagnerian repertoire on today's operatic stage. Operagoers compare her talents with those of such predecessors as Kirsten Flagstad, Lilli Lehmann, and that other famous Swedish Nilsson, Christine, who sang hereabouts in the 1870's. Not that anybody who is familiar with Birgit Nilsson's singing actually remembers Christine's or Lilli Lehmann's, but opera buffs write, read, and hand down as oral tradition an enormous amount of information concerning the exact specifications of the voices of great singers. And just as they were doing it in Christine Nilsson's time, so they are doing it today in regard to Birgit Nilsson. To begin with, she is widely conceded to be the greatest contemporary Wagnerian soprano, belonging to the rare type that is likely to turn up only once or twice in a generation, at most. To say that she is Mademoiselle Flagstad's successor is true as far as it goes. But Miss Nilsson has her own claims to preeminence. Not only has she sung all the roles that Mademoiselle Flagstad was famous for, but she has added to them a large repertoire of other roles, German and Italian, which she sings with equal success. She is not only the greatest living Brünnhilde and Isolde but also the greatest living Leonore, Salome, Elektra, and Turandot, and she is certainly one of the greatest Aidas and Amelias (in Verdi's *Un Ballo in Maschera*). Such a wide range of roles has probably not been encompassed by any single singer since Lilli Lehmann, and there will undoubtedly be more roles to come. Miss Nilsson has, moreover, a record of dependability—of uniformly splendid performances—that can be matched by few other prima donnas. She has, in fact, no rivals at all. She is the indispensable soprano—not only at the Metropolitan, but at La Scala, the Vienna State Opera, the Deutsche Oper, in West Berlin, and Bayreuth.

It goes without saying that this extraordinary eminence rests primarily on a remarkable voice—one that, as a purely physical mechanism, is built on a heroic scale. It can outshout the most massive Wagnerian orchestrations with ease, competing with batteries of trumpets and trombones. Its range is large, reaching up to an effortless D-flat, and even beyond. (Miss Nilsson is said to be able to sing E's and F's in private, but she sings no roles demanding these notes.) She deliberately changes the quality of her voice for different roles—from the girlish soprano of her Salome and the brilliant, somewhat strident trumpeting of her Princess Turandot to the rich, warm, passionate delivery required for the Wagner heroines. A few years ago, when she did the vocal stunt of appearing as both Venus and Elisabeth in the same performance of *Tannhäuser*, her voice seemed to be that of two different women. As happens only with the most celebrated singers, her singing never betrays any sense of strain; on the contrary, the listener always has a feeling that there are immense reserves of power and range. Moreover, her voice, like some others of this weight and power, tends to lighten in quality and to gain in elasticity as a performance progresses. Miss Nilsson has never attempted to sing Bellini's *Norma*, because of the agility that the role requires ("Too many little notes," she says), but she has conceded that she might have sung it if the florid aria "Casta diva" came at the end of the opera instead of at the beginning. Actually, just for the fun of it, she once sang the Queen of the Night's aria from the second act of Mozart's *Die Zauberflöte* (ordinarily the province of the highest and most agile coloratura sopranos) *after* she had appeared as Brünnhilde in *Götterdämmerung*. This feat was performed in her dressing room for a few friends, and was later reported to the conductor Karl Böhm. Böhm refused to believe that it had ever happened, so Miss Nilsson, always ready to take on a challenge and rout a disbeliever, did it again, after her next *Götterdämmerung;* this time Mr. Böhm himself, somewhat stunned, was at the piano. Miss Nilsson would never, of course, attempt the role in an opera house; it *could* be done, she once explained to a friend, but it would require about three hours of strenuous warming up beforehand, and she simply hasn't the time for that sort of thing.

Miss Nilsson, in fact, hasn't much time for anything except singing. Her schedule of performances takes up all but a few scattered weeks of any given year. She is in demand continuously in, among other places, Milan, Rome, Bayreuth, Berlin, San Francisco, Buenos Aires, and what she calls "my home base"— Stockholm. The relatively long spell of two and a half months that she spends in New York annually is a tribute partly to the Metropolitan's prestige and affluence and partly to the fact that New York has what she calls "a fine climate." Like many singers, Miss Nilsson has an almost superstitious horror of fresh air, because of its supposedly damaging effect on the larynx, and she is one of the very few people who breathe New York's polluted air with gratification. "Who knows that it isn't good for you?" she once said to an acquaintance. "I love it." She regards her stay in New York as a relatively serene experience, since most of the rest of her year is spent rushing from one place to another, always by plane. She has no home, other than a succession of hotels. She does have a husband—a Swedish businessman named Bertil Niklasson—whom she sees when her schedule permits. ("I cannot be an artist and have a home. You have to say 'No, thank you' to either one. I say 'No, thank you' to a home. I love my profession so much, and my husband is so understanding.") She and Mr. Niklasson maintain an apartment in Stockholm and one in Paris. She has few friends (most of them are also singers), and virtually no intimate ones ("nobody I tell my secrets to"). Her time is so neatly divided among performances, rehearsals, the study of new roles, and plane trips that she has almost no leisure. For a week or two at Christmas, she goes home to Västra Karup, the village in southern Sweden where she was born, to visit her father, who runs a farm there. These Christmas visits are her only regular vacations, and she usually sings several times in the local church in the course of them. The fact is that Miss Nilsson doesn't like vacations of any length, because, as she put it the other day, "if you rest too long, it is harder to bring the voice back into shape."

Miss Nilsson takes her nomadic existence in stride, and she takes her fame that way, too. She has no entourage of admirers—no fan clubs. Once she expressed to Mrs. Geraldine Souvaine, who runs the intermission radio shows for the Metropolitan broadcasts, a certain diffidence about giving away the two complimentary tickets that had been allotted to her for a performance of *Turandot*. "It is very embarrassing to have to *ask* people to come and hear me sing," she said. "I cannot do it." On the other hand, she is delighted to have people *pay* to hear her sing, and she is well known in opera circles for demanding, and getting, the highest fee that any opera house offers. She undoubtedly makes more money in a year than any other living singer, even though she sings in a good many opera houses, like Bayreuth and Vienna, where the fees are not particularly high. It is apparently not so much the money itself that attracts her as it is the money as an index to public interest in her singing. She regards her work, very simply, as a business, and her voice as an exploitable commodity of specific value. Miss Nilsson measures roles as a taximeter measures miles. She can tell you instantly exactly how many bars there are for Isolde to sing (seventeen hundred and fifty), and exactly how many minutes she has to stand up during the first act (seventy-eight). She knows the precise dimensions of all her roles, and is quick to correct anybody who compliments her inaccurately, saying something like "How marvelous that you could sing Isolde and Tosca in the same week!" "Don't forget the Leonore in between," she is apt to retort. When Karl Böhm once remarked, "You are the greatest Brünnhilde I have heard in forty years," Miss Nilsson immediately asked, "And who did you hear forty years ago?" Mr. Böhm couldn't think of anybody. Several years ago she wrote from Helsinki to a New York acquaintance in her slam-bang English:

"I hate working now after "Elektra." I gave everything there [in Stockholm], so now I just feel I want a vacation instead. We were down in Southsweden for 4 days and that only made the appetite worse. Those idiots at UPI or AP. They wrote that we had 20 minutes applause after "Elektra." It was exactly *32* minutes. And then I got a clipping from Dallas about "Elektra" where they say I am 48. Is not the real situation [barely forty-seven at the time] bad enough? This UPI or AP is just as bad as *Time,* which always lies about my age, to please I don't know what other prima donna!

In another letter (she is a compulsive letter writer), she wrote, "51 curtain calls after 'Tristan'! Record both for me and Hamburg." From Vienna:

Yesterday we had "Tristan" here and it was a great, great performance. I was actually in super-voice. We got *50* curtain calls, 15 after Act I and II, and 25 after the last one. Ah boy! It really makes 55!! There, you see, how bad I am in counting. I have to look over my fees again. Maybe I counted them wrong, too.

Unlike other prima donnas, Miss Nilsson likes to make all her contractual arrangements herself. She rarely has to haggle over terms, since her unique position is a commanding one at any conference with an impresario. She has no manager, saying, "I am too independable to have a manager. Besides, I don't like being put on and taken off planes like luggage." She enjoys the byplay that occurs in impresarios' offices while they are trying to secure her services. Once she was negotiating a contract with Herbert Von Karajan, at the time director of the Vienna Opera, when a string of pearls she was wearing broke and scattered all over the floor. Von Karajan and several others who were present got down on their knees to search for the pearls. "We must find every one of them," Von Karajan said. "These are the expensive pearls that Miss Nilsson buys with her high fees from the Metropolitan." "No," Miss Nilsson replied. "These are just imitation ones, which I buy with my low fees from the Vienna Opera." Once a contract is drawn up, Miss Nilsson writes the date of her engagement down in a little black book that she keeps in her purse. The book contains dates for performances as far ahead as three years, and it is her only record. But she has never missed an engagement.

Miss Nilsson not only does her own managing but learns all her new roles by herself (most divas have to be coached), often in hotels and on plane trips. (She also makes her own travel arrangements.) She is an accomplished musician, able to read at sight, and she can learn a role silently while sitting almost anywhere, even among throngs of people. Once a role has been read and memorized, it sticks in her mind indelibly; indeed, she cannot read it in a different edition without becoming confused. Her memory is photographic; certain notes appear at certain places on the page and remain there in her mind permanently. And she sets her own standards, knowing exactly how good or how faulty her singing has been at any given performance. As a corollary, she is absolutely impervious to flattery. She is happy to be praised if she knows that she deserves it, otherwise not; if there is anything she loathes, it is being confronted by somebody who insists on all the hand-kissing and dispensing of adulation that most prima donnas thrive on. As a recording-company executive recently remarked, "She can spot a phony a mile further off than anybody else I know."

Perhaps the most impressive thing about Miss Nilsson's determined do-it-yourself professional attitude is that she is almost completely self-taught as a singer. She had some singing lessons as a young girl in Västra Karup, and she had some valuable training in strictly musical matters at the Royal School of Music in Stockholm. But in those days she was without the high notes that she has now. Nobody told her about what singers refer to as "support." She discovered that all by herself one night when she was trying to devise a means of singing while suffering from a bad cold. She found a way to make her voice float over the cold, and shortly thereafter she discovered that she could sing in upper regions that

113

were entirely new. She is methodical in caring for her voice, and she has a rapid method of warming it up before a performance. The process takes about three to four minutes, and those who have heard it describe it as sounding perfectly awful. But it works. She has never been known to "clam up" or miss a note. As she says, "Always when I open my mouth, something comes out. I was born with strong things in my throat." Being supremely confident of her vocal powers, Miss Nilsson has had rows with various conductors from time to time. "I like to have suggestions, but I also like a conductor who is with us on the stage," she told an interviewer. "I like to see a smiling face down there." Once, she wrote her New York friend from Europe:

> 56 curtain calls after "Tristan." The conductor was so-so. He killed my "Liebestod" by taking it 4 times as fast as usual. It was more like a sort of Polonaise. . . . Then we had "Turandot" two days later, and it was wonderful. Someone else conducted. He may not be a second Toscanini, but after the first one he was like a god. I kissed him in front of the curtain, showing how happy I was to have a real conductor. We had 60 curtains calls that night.

Her position is that she *knows* how to sing and will take full responsibility for the vocal side of any role she appears in. As for the dramatic side, she feels it is the duty of others to provide scenery, coordination, and help. Miss Nilsson has great reverence for good stage directors, and she follows their suggestions with humility and admiration. Her favorite man in this field was the late Wieland Wagner, grandson of Richard and director at Bayreuth and elsewhere. Asked what she admired most about Herr Wagner, she replied that he had a fantastic imagination and that, having once been a painter, he had an uncanny way of handling lighting. ("He could make people look sixteen or seventeen just by changing the lights.") Moreover, he treated each singer as an individual, and knew what each could do best. He created an Isolde for Miss Nilsson that was completely different from Bayreuth's two other

Isoldes—Astrid Varnay's and Martha Mödl's. "He had a great understanding for singers," she said. "There are not too many good stage directors." She carries around with her a small photograph of a rare drawing of Richard Wagner, which his grandson presented to her, and she once paid Wieland the highest compliment in the Nilsson vocabulary. "I get down on my nose to him," she told a group of acquaintances.

Because the world today is not rich in the always rare commodity of true Wagnerian heldentenors—and is not even particularly rich in great tenors of any sort—Miss Nilsson's appearances are often disturbingly overweighted by her own vocal brilliance. Since the retirement of Lauritz Melchior, there has been no Wagnerian tenor with the kind of power it takes to compete with a voice like hers. In most European opera houses—like Bayreuth, Vienna, and Paris—which are smaller than the ones in this country, this is not so much of a problem. Wolfgang Windgassen, the German tenor who is frequently her partner in Europe, has a voice that is capable of filling auditoriums with a capacity of two thousand people or less, but at the old Metropolitan, which was nearly twice as big, he was not quite as effective. (The new Met holds about the same number of people.) Miss Nilsson is a very good friend of Mr. Windgassen's, especially because of an incident in Florence about ten years ago. The opera was *Siegfried*, and Windgassen, in the title role, had just discovered Miss Nilsson, as Brünnhilde, sleeping on the mountaintop within the circle of magic fire. As Miss Nilsson rose from her bed of rock, she had a feeling that her costume, which hooked up the back, was awfully loose. It had just been to the cleaners, and, for some reason, all the hooks and eyes had come apart. Being a good trouper, she resolutely faced the audience and hoped for a miracle. At this point, Windgassen discovered what was wrong, put his arms around her, and managed to do up some of the hooks. It saved the evening for Miss Nilsson, and she has been grateful ever since. Another of her good friends is a tenor who doesn't appear in Wagnerian opera. He is Franco Corelli, and he

115

Miss Nilsson as Lady Macbeth
in *Macbeth*. *Photograph by Hiro*

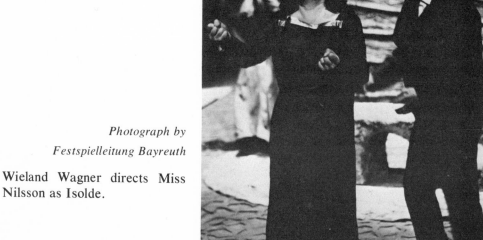

Photograph by
Festspielleitung Bayreuth

Wieland Wagner directs Miss
Nilsson as Isolde.

Birgit Nilsson shows her husband, Bertil Niklasson, a doll replica of Brünnhilde made by a fan.

Miss Nilsson's official debut at the Stockholm Opera as Lady Macbeth in Verdi's *Macbeth* with Sigurd Björling.

Miss Nilsson as Brünnhilde.

Rehearsing *Aida* with conductor Georg Solti at the Met.

comes near to being her equal on the stage for the simple reason that he is the only existing tenor who can shout almost as loud as she can. Their association, which began in Italy prior to their first appearances at the Metropolitan, did not start under the most favorable circumstances. At La Scala, Miss Nilsson was cast as Princess Turandot and Mr. Corelli as Calaf, the hero of Puccini's opera—two roles into which the composer built a certain element of competition. Miss Nilsson is ordinarily the most cooperative of singers, but when anybody tries to outdo her, she instinctively rises to the challenge. (In Italy, this habit has earned her the title *la voce di vendetta*, or "the revenge voice.") Mr. Corelli is justly proud of having the most magnificent voice of its type to be heard nowadays in Italian opera, and he is not exactly reticent about showing it off. There is an aria—or, properly speaking, a duet—in the second act of *Turandot* called "In questa reggia," in which a certain high C is taken by both soprano and tenor and is often held just for the bravura effect. Mr. Corelli started by holding this note longer than Miss Nilsson, which, with Miss Nilsson, was a tactical mistake. At the next performance, she held the note until Mr. Corelli was out of breath, and then some. Later, according to a story that has become legendary, the two appeared in *Turandot* in Boston on a Metropolitan Opera tour. On this occasion, Mr. Corelli, after having been thoroughly outshouted in "In questa reggia," immediately left the stage (he had no more to sing, but he was supposed to be there), sulked in his dressing room, and declared that he would not come out again. At this point, Rudolf Bing is said to have entered the dressing room with an idea wonderfully calculated to appeal to the tenor's *amour propre*. "In America, a man cannot retreat before a woman," Mr. Bing is reported to have said. "Continue! And in the last act, when the time comes to kiss her, *bite* her instead." Mr. Corelli is said to have followed instructions, and Mr. Bing, according to the story, fled to New York, where Miss Nilsson telephoned him, saying, "I cannot go on to Cleveland. I have rabies." There is still a commonly held notion that every performance of *Turandot* with Nilsson and Corelli contains a vocal duel to the death. If so, it is a friendly duel. Nowadays, Mr. Corelli is very ready with enormous bunches of roses for Miss Nilsson, and she, for her part, has long since admitted that Mr. Corelli is the only tenor who is in her class at playing the game of opera. She admires him, he admires her, and the Nilsson-Corelli combination has gone on to sing *Tosca*.

Competitiveness and heroism seem to be deeply embedded in Miss Nilsson's character. According to an impresario who has dealt with her frequently, she competes against illness by singing better when she doesn't feel well than when she does. Her first Aida of the 1963-64 Metropolitan season—a huge success—was done following a sleepless night during which she was in acute pain from some internal trouble. She competes against the past by trying to outdo her famous predecessors—and often succeeds. Her ambition in this respect seems to exceed that of most prima donnas, and, even taking into consideration her love of prestige and adding a mystical ingredient of Viking blood, one doesn't arrive at a convincing explanation of it. But if one remembers that Miss Nilsson is an entirely self-made diva and a former farm girl who escaped from farm life and would rather die than go back to it, one has perhaps an inkling of what has driven her to her strenuous achievements. In an interview some time ago, she described her father, Nils Svensson, as a crusty old farmer in the rich country sixty miles north of Malmo, in southern Sweden. Nils Svensson at least pretended that he had absolutely no interest in whether his daughter was a great diva or not. He is completely unmusical, and he hates to travel. He has heard his daughter sing only a few times and then only in Stockholm or over radio or television. As Miss Nilsson herself explained it, "He is stubborn, like me— *more* stubborn than I am. He has a terribly strong will—but he has a sense of humor. He is a comedian—but he thinks farming is more important than singing." Nils Svensson was not a man to be unduly impressed by city folk and their outlandish preoccupations.

When he was asked, as frequently happened, how it felt to be the father of one of the world's most famous prima donnas, his usual reply was "Fine, fine. Why *shouldn't* she be a famous prima donna? Look at all the money that was spent on her training." (As a matter of fact, Miss Nilsson has been too proud to accept a cent from her father, since she knows that he disapproved of her career.) At one of her Stockholm performances, while she was taking a bow to enthusiastic applause, her father made quite a show of shushing those around him, saying, "Why do you applaud? It's only my daughter." One of his favorite habits at her performances at the Royal Opera was to walk up and down in the lobby during the intermission, buttonholing strangers and saying, "What do you really think? I think she was too loud, don't you?" Most disagreed with him, but finally, by a process of elimination, he came across somebody who fell in with his opinion. He was then beside himself with satisfaction, and after the performance he greeted his daughter with the triumphant statement "Everybody thought you were too loud."

This sort of teasing has been going on ever since Miss Nilsson's childhood. She was born in Västra Karup not, as some people believe, in a log cabin but in the Svensson home, a fairly imposing farmhouse. Märta Birgit Nilsson, as she was named (Swedes sometimes take their father's first name as their last), turned out to be an only child, and her father, reasoning that if she could not be a male and take over the farm, which had been in the family for many generations, she could at least be a farmer's wife, sent her to agricultural school, where she learned to milk cows and cook. But, as often happens in the households of dominating men, there was a quiet but determined resistance on the scene, in this case Birgit's mother, née Justina Pålsson. Mrs. Svensson didn't particularly like being a farm woman; she had always wanted to be a singer, and she did a great deal of singing at parties among friends. (She died some years ago, and Miss Nilsson remembers that she could sing high C's at the age of sixty.) By the time Birgit was three years old, her mother had got her a toy piano, on which Birgit very quickly managed to pick out the notes of all the melodies she had heard. Later her father himself bought an old-fashioned pedal-pump organ, on which she learned to perform while her mother worked the pedals that she could not reach. Even during her cooking and cow-milking period, Birgit was singing in the choir of the local church. At fifteen, she timidly entered a competition for vocal instruction at the nearby resort town of Båstad—"a nice place, where even our King goes in summer" is how she describes it. The man who was holding these auditions was Ragnar Blennow, a church organist and choirmaster (the Swedish title for this is "cantor") who worked in the neighborhood. Blennow accepted her as a pupil, and at her very first lesson he said, "You are going to be a great singer." "He never said it again, though," Miss Nilsson recalled the other day, and for many years she remained pessimistic about her vocal powers. The height of her ambition at the time was to be a church singer. But Cantor Blennow turned out to be that great rarity, a fine vocal teacher. He taught Miss Nilsson for several years and was, in fact, the first and the last vocal teacher she had. Meanwhile, Miss Nilsson's mother, who had saved the equivalent of five hundred dollars from an inheritance, was making plans to send her to the Royal School of Music in Stockholm in spite of her father's disapproval. At the appropriate time, Birgit was bundled off with the five hundred dollars and a high recommendation from Cantor Blennow. Her father refused to contribute a cent and viewed the whole business with disgust. Not only had he had the bad fortune to be deprived of a son who could take over the farm, but now his daughter, who had been trained to farm and might have married a man capable of pursuing the family tradition, was being taken away from him. Miss Nilsson was happy to get away, but people who know the family maintain that she has been trying to convince her father ever since that being a world-famous diva makes up, at least in part, for having failed to be first a son and then a farmer's wife. Whatever the truth of this view, Miss Nilsson

123

has remained close to her father, visiting him as often as her busy schedule permits. She has made many improvements in the old farmhouse, which, to judge from photographs that she carries around with her, now resembles a well-kept home on a country estate. It was never, of course, a particularly humble place. Västra Karup is in the province of Skåne, which is the Wisconsin of Sweden, having—as Miss Nilsson remarked recently, with all the authority of a born agriculturist—"very good ground." Skåne produces a large part of the cheeses, butter, and other dairy products that Sweden consumes, and Miss Nilsson maintains that its inhabitants, who were under Danish rule as late as three hundred years ago and who speak a dialect that has Danish expressions in it, are different from other Swedes. "We are not dull," she says. "We have more sense of humor than most Swedes." In addition to the Italian, German, and English that her operatic career has required her to learn, Miss Nilsson speaks both true Swedish and the native Skåne dialect, which she uses when talking with her father, and also with her husband, who comes from the same region.

Miss Nilsson approached the Royal School of Music with some trepidation, and sang Elisabeth's Prayer, from *Tannhäuser,* at her entrance examination. It was one of two or three operatic arias she had learned. She was accepted, and a year later she was awarded the Christine Nilsson Scholarship, which provided for her tuition. For living expenses, once her mother's five hundred dollars had run out, she worked as a church singer at funerals and as a chorus singer with various oratorio groups. The Royal School in Stockholm is one of the finest musical conservatories of its sort in the world, and Sweden has produced great singers in a number altogether disproportionate to its population, including such figures of international operatic history as Jenny Lind, Christine Nilsson, Nanny Larsén-Todsen, Karin Branzell, Göta Ljungberg, Set Svanholm, and Jussi Björling, as well as many less celebrated but very able artists. It confers a degree, and any singer who attains it graduates almost automatically into the Royal Opera. In nearly all cases, being a good student at this institution results in a distinguished career. But Miss Nilsson was, as she recently expressed it, "too independable" to be a submissive student. In the first place, she thought that a vocal teacher there was about to ruin her voice, and, in the second, the piano teacher infuriated her. In view of her special talents, she was permitted to drop out of her vocal classes and continue to train herself by the methods that Cantor Blennow had taught her. She had to go on with the piano classes, however, and also master the better part of a curriculum that included solfeggio, harmony, languages (Italian and German), and diction. Much of her present keen musicianship and ability to teach herself new roles is the result of this thorough early training. Vocally, however, she remained self-taught from that time on. And to this day Miss Nilsson has a distrust of the whole voice-teaching profession. Somebody once remarked to her that one day she herself would make a great teacher. She was horrified at the thought. "I do not have the patience," she said. "Anyway, as a teacher I would only have two or three things to say. And there is the terrible responsibility. Most vocal teachers have to make a living. I don't blame them. But they encourage young people who have no talent, and bring in them great hopes. This is very bad. If they tell you you have no future, they are doing you a favor, but they don't do it."

Miss Nilsson's operatic debut took place in Stockholm in 1946, when another singer fell ill, leaving a sudden vacancy in the role of Agathe in *Der Freischütz*. This early German romantic opera, which is seldom heard in America, calls for some arias and some spoken dialogue and recitatives from its heroine. Miss Nilsson knew the arias but not what went on between them, and though she boned up rapidly on the intervening material, she was far from thoroughly prepared when the time came. On the way to the Royal Opera for the performance, she became so frightened and depressed that while she was crossing a bridge, she contemplated jumping into the water. "I was *really* scared," she recalled. Sure enough, she made a couple of mistakes during the performance, and the conductor, Leo Blech—one of those violent German disciplinarians—had her temporarily banned from the opera stage. "I thought I was finished," Miss Nilsson said. The next year, a more benign German conductor, Fritz Busch, came to Stockholm and engaged her for the role of Lady Macbeth in Verdi's opera. The end of the sleepwalking scene in this opera involves Lady Macbeth in a big dramatic aria that finishes on a high D-flat as she walks offstage. Busch, perhaps following the tradition of some of Germany's lesser opera houses, proposed that Miss Nilsson leave the D-flat to another singer, behind the scenes. (As Miss Nilsson has pointed out, the whole arrangement was ridiculous. It is harder to sing that D-flat from a standing start than it is to sing the whole aria and the D-flat, too.) At rehearsals, the other singer cracked the note several times, and finally Miss Nilsson went to the conductor and said, "Mr. Busch, I will be blamed if that note is cracked anyhow. Why not let me crack my own D-flat?" Mr. Busch agreed, and Miss Nilsson sang a number of performances complete with the D-flat and never cracked it once. These performances were really her start as a diva. She was soon considered the most promising young luminary of the Royal Opera and sang a large variety of roles in German and Italian opera.

Her first important appearance outside Sweden was at the Glyndebourne Festival in England, where in 1951, she sang Electra in Mozart's *Idomeneo*. Shortly afterward, however, she had a bout of pleurisy that kept her off the stage for a year. Such attacks are not unknown among singers, and fortunately Miss Nilsson returned to opera refreshed rather than damaged, though for many months she had to limit the number of her appearances. By 1954, she had made debuts in Vienna and in Bayreuth, where she sang Elsa in *Lohengrin*, returning later on to sing the more demanding roles of Brünnhilde and Isolde. It was also in 1954 that she received the Swedish title of *Hovsångerska*, or Singer to the

Royal Court. In 1956, the enterprising impresario of the San Francisco Opera, Kurt Herbert Adler, engaged her for her American operatic debut. (She had sung in this country previously only at a concert in the Hollywood Bowl.) Mr. Bing, of the Metropolitan, had so far turned her down. She had sung an audition for him in Berlin and failed, and later he heard her do Salome in Munich and again decided against hiring her. Naturally, she was disappointed. It was not until 1958, when he heard her as Isolde at the Vienna Opera (an institution that Mr. Bing appeared to consider the indispensable training school for Metropolitan singers), that he offered her a contract. Her Metropolitan debut the following year was greeted with front-page reviews in the daily press and was widely regarded as the most important event of its sort since the debut of Kirsten Flagstad, in 1935. Asked about her reaction to Mr. Bing's rather dilatory approach, she said, "I was not mad. I develop slowly. I was glad to come to the Metropolitan when my voice was better. But," she added, characteristically, "if Mr. Bing had hired me then, I might not have been so expensive."

Miss Nilsson, being a great self-improver, can be counted on to sing each role better every season. She restudies constantly, and people who have worked with her say that, given a couple of months between performances of a particular role, she will always return to it with improvements, both vocal and dramatic. Her voice has grown in warmth during the later part of her career and she explains this phenomenon by noting that when she was younger she had to push her voice in order to make it adequate to the big Wagnerian roles. "When you push," she says, "the voice becomes white." But Miss Nilsson, for all her experience and fame, is still not without her attacks of nerves. Before her first double appearance as Elisabeth and Venus in *Tannhäuser*, she spent a completely sleepless night, and her description of it will be familiar to many insomniacs: "First I couldn't sleep. Then I got worried that I wouldn't get any sleep. Then I got mad at myself for not sleeping. So I *didn't* get any sleep. Sometimes I am so stupid I hate myself." She has also had some experiences on the stage that would unhinge the average actor. She described one of these in a letter to her New York friend. Dated London, April 14, 1962, it began:

Friday 13th, yesterday, was the premiere of "Tristan & Isolde," and it was really the 13th. Between the general rehearsal and the premiere, they spreaded my costume in a green color. It was a nice color indeed. I jumped in my costume in the last minute and found that the nice new color made me green *all* over. The overture began and I went on the stage in *tears!* My hands were after 5 minutes so dark green that I could not see the difference between them and my clothes. Brangäne became green, Tristan almost all-over green, and I was at the end of the act green as a tree from tip to bottom. Ah boy! I have still no idea what I did on the stage. . . . The second act was better, because I changed dress, but then I got the green color back from Tristan in the long love duet, because there had been no costume change for him. *That was Friday 13th!* P.S. The man who spreaded my costume cried also. He had used water color instead of—I do not know what. But it was quite a mistake.

Another letter, also from London, and dated September 2, 1963, is eloquent about the trials of a working soprano:

I am enclosing a picture from the painting that is finally ready. [The King of Sweden had commissioned a portrait of her.] I stood in pose 33 hours, sometimes 6 hours a day. I would prefer to sing 2 Isoldes in one day than to pose for 6 hours. Ah boy! I sang at a concert in the museum the same night the painting was shown for the first time. It is, as I said before, going to hang at Gripsholm Castle, where many prominent Swedish persons are hanging—kings etc., but only 2 female singers before me: Jenny Lind and Christine Nilsson. . . . On my 100th Isolde, in Bayreuth, I got 100 roses, and from Wolfgang and Wieland Wagner a portrait of old Richard. I am writing this letter backstage at Covent Garden, while waiting for my entrance in the first act of "Götterdämmerung." It is orchestra rehearsal, and it takes such a long time. If I come to New York still alive and with both legs in good shape, I'll be more than happy. The stage here is like this so I wish I had fly-feets. There is a very small place where we can be secure. All over the stage are empty spaces. If you put down your foot there, you'll never see it any more. . . . Then we have a spotlight in our eyes, so we cannot see where we are walking, *only feel.* I wonder what the next genius designer will make. Maybe I'll have to hang on one foot 20 meters over the stage while I am singing the Nile aria from "Aida."

Miss Nilsson has once or twice been in a position to correct what she conceived to be bad stage design—at least where her own costume and makeup were concerned. For the Metropolitan's production of *Turandot*—one of the splashiest and most elaborate spectacles ever presented in the old opera house—Cecil Beaton, the designer, had specified special, very thick makeup in order to give everybody a Chinese-doll look. To begin with, Miss Nilsson never liked Mr. Beaton's scenery for this opera, and when it came to the thick makeup, she would have none of it after the initial performance. She made herself up as she thought she should look, appeared that way, and has never seen any reason to change her mind since.

Generally, Miss Nilsson's backstage relations are very good. Her colleagues like her, and she often invites them to dinner at her apartment in the Hotel Alden, where she puts on a huge white apron and cooks for them. She has been a good cook ever since her days in agricultural school, and she insists on doing everything for her guests, refusing even to let them help her with the dishes. There in Swedish. She generally sticks to her hotel room in her leisure hours, often cooking her own meals. She is in touch with her husband in Stockholm by telephone nearly every day. On those rare occasions when she is "at home," in Västra Karup, she goes swimming or horseback riding, and she is a great walker wherever she is. She hates cold weather and sometimes flies to Florida for a weekend while she is working at the Metropolitan. But most of the time, as she said recently, "when I don't sing, I eat or sleep," adding, "I cannot think of anything I would like more than being a singer."

Yet she is not always so sanguine. Her Elektra, which was unveiled in 1966, caused her a certain amount of concern. In the first place, she considers it the most difficult role she has ever sung. "If it is uncut, it has about fifteen hundred measures, and you have to sing loud all the time," she says. "I'm not sure it's good for my voice. Isolde has seventeen hundred and fifty measures, but you can relax part of the time. Elektra never relaxes. Isolde is not difficult, if you have comfortable shoes." As is her custom with a new role, she sang Elektra in Stockholm and then in Vienna before appearing in it in New York. This was a precautionary procedure. She doesn't want to bring anything to the Metropolitan until she is sure it is polished to perfection. As she explained it, "If you make a big success in New York, it goes all over; if you make a big flop, it goes all over, too." Prior to her Stockholm *Elektra*, she wrote her New York friend:

Finalmente a sign that I am still alive. You have no idea how busy I have been. I have even cutted my hair myself, because I never found time for a hairdresser. When I came home at Easter . . . I only knew one scene from "Elektra" by heart. Then I was almost working 20 hours a day to keep up with the stage director, because I did not want to show him how little I knew. After 3 days he caught me in the last duet, which I had to sing with the score in my hand. Well, despite of all the work it has been a marvellous time, and I have enjoyed it very much.

[Then, from Bayreuth]:

I have got a lot of pain in my neck and shoulders. Probably from driving cars. It hurts very much. I was at the hospital in Sweden and got an injection in my left shoulder and it helped a great lot. But now I have got it in my right, and with pain in my head. Ah boy! Why do I have such a profession, where nobody cares about my lovely shoulders, only about my voice. . . . Regarding what that man writes about my Elektra in Stockholm, I am glad that he raved so, but what does he think the dance should be like? As soon as some Americans see it is a dance, they think it should be something sexy. Elektra was *no* dancer—not like Salome—and she is at the end of her life. She feels the rhythms and she is lifting her legs in the Greek style. That you can see on all paintings, vases, etc., but she has no force and no knowledges to make a *beautiful* dance. It should be in a more grotesque way. Well I know those people who want everything sexy; they do not even know what that word means, *poveri!* I was once complimented on the sexy draperies in my apartment. Well, I'll try, of course, to change it so the Yankees will like it, too, when I come to New York.

In the spring of 1972 she sang Elektra for the first time at La Scala. They gave her a new production. It was the one hundred and twelfth new production that has been given her during her career—a record probably unmatched by any other singer in history. An interviewer once asked Miss Nilsson, "If you had six months of complete freedom, with no singing schedule whatever, what would you do?" Miss Nilsson seemed taken aback for a moment. Obviously, the idea had never occurred to her before. She thought over the question earnestly and then replied, "I would like to travel. There are so many things to see." In response to a look of incredulity, she quickly added, "You do not understand. There are many cities in the world where I have seen only the airport, the inside of my hotel room, the inside of a taxi, and the inside of the opera house. Sometime I am going to go sightseeing, like other people."

are two sopranos, however—and only two—with whom her relations are somewhat ruffled. One is Joan Sutherland, who, of course, can claim to be a rival for the title of "world's greatest soprano," though she is a totally different kind of singer and doesn't appear in the roles that Miss Nilsson plays. The other is Renata Tebaldi— and the ruffled feelings in this case are apparently due to a misunderstanding. Once, when Miss Tebaldi was singing in *Tosca*, Miss Nilsson stood in the wings admiringly, thinking that she was, so to speak, cheering the other great soprano on. But Miss Tebaldi, seeing her there, came to the conclusion that Miss Nilsson was gloating over some shortcoming or other. Ever since, Miss Tebaldi has maintained that Miss Nilsson has *il malocchio,* or "the evil eye," and solemnly crosses herself whenever Miss Nilsson is around. Miss Nilsson herself is neither religious nor superstitious. Swedish friends of hers explain that few people in Sweden are really religious, though the Swedes are nominally Lutherans. They blame this lack of religion on the religious instruction in Swedish schools. "We start with the Old Testament and we go very slowly and methodically," one of them remarked. "By the time we reach the New Testament, it is too late." But Miss Nilsson has a casual interest in astrology, mainly derived from her discovery that she is Taurus and has a lot of the characteristics that go with that sign. "Many great singers have been Taurus," she once said. "We have our feet planted on the ground. We have thick necks and loud voices, and we are clever about money. I don't take it all very seriously, but sometimes I think there is something to it."

Miss Nilsson may be clever about money, but the people around her have often wondered what she does with the large amounts of it that she makes. Even she admits that spending money is a problem for one who leads such a restless existence. She is an avid shopper in whatever city she happens to be in, but her purchases are usually limited to portable objects, such as jewelry and clothes. She has, however, a consuming passion for Persian rugs, which she has wrapped up and sent to Paris, where she has a large collection of them. Some people maintain that she sings in Vienna mainly because that city has one of the most famous auction houses in the world—the Dorotheum. Miss Nilsson admits that she never goes to Vienna without visiting the place, and that she was once late for a performance of *Salome* at the Vienna Opera because she spent too long at the Dorotheum bidding on a very special Persian rug. She got it, but because she was in a hurry, she offered a very high bid to

Because of her restless mode of life, Miss Nilsson is a great connoisseur of hotels, and she has ironclad tastes. From Vienna she wrote her New York friend some time ago. "I cannot stand this hotel anymore. My room has read walls, read carpet, and cristal lamps. I feel like something between the Marschallin and a 'Bordell-frau.' I see read wherever I go. I get headaches from the color." The hotels she favors are always quiet ones. "I can't stand lively hotels," she says. "People are always giving parties and leaving the door open. I have to sleep." Among her favorite hotels are the Hassler in Rome, the Huntington in San Francisco, the Franklin Park in Washington, the Continental in Milan, and the Grand in Paris. When she is by herself, which is a good deal of the time, Miss Nilsson reads, writes letters, or does crossword puzzles discourage all the competition, and she feels that she paid too much. Such pressures of time and events are all part of the life of a jetpropelled working soprano. As another instance, Miss Nilsson recalls a stay in Buenos Aires during the revolution against the Perón dictatorship. "They were shooting all over," she says. "My husband was with me that trip, and we stayed in the hotel eating ham sandwiches and playing cards. I had all our suitcases packed, but we couldn't get out, because the elevators didn't work and the bellboys were all out in the revolution. I was very scared. After it was over, there were effigies of Perón hanging from all the trees, and the people were shouting, 'Viva Libertad! Viva Wagner! Viva Nilsson!'"

DILWORTH

Photograph by Hubert Dilworth

Miss Price as Donna Anna in Mozart's *Don Giovanni* at the Met.

V

Leontyne Price

Photograph by Alix Jeffry

Leontyne Price at home, seated in front of her portrait, painted by Bradley Phillips.

In 1955, in what was probably his most important innovation, Rudolf Bing integrated the Metropolitan Opera. Why the step had not been taken before remains a mystery. But at last America's great reservoir of black singing talent could be tapped at America's leading opera house. The first break in the all-white tradition came tentatively. The great black mezzo-soprano Marian Anderson, by that time way past her peak as a vocalist but still the most famous of black singers, made a debut at the Met in the unglamorous role of Ulrica, the fortune-teller, in Verdi's *Un Ballo in Maschera*. She did not sing brilliantly; it was too late in her career. But the gesture had been made, and the audience applauded wildly. From that occasion onward, a fine succession of black singers became regular parts of Metropolitan casts. That same year, a black baritone named Robert McFerrin appeared, only to disappear from the operatic stage a short time afterward. The following year the scintillating black coloratura soprano Mattiwilda Dobbs made a huge success, and later went off to live in Europe. She was followed two years later by Gloria Davy, a fine lyric soprano who also fled to Europe after a few seasons. So far the Met seemed able to present a black singer for a season or two, but seemed unable to retain one after a reputation had been made and a European career was possible. Most black singers preferred Europe because there was no racial problem there, and a couple of the Met's black alumni subsequently married whites across the Atlantic.

By 1959 a black soprano named Martina Arroyo was hired for smaller roles, and Miss Arroyo, unlike her predecessors, remained with the institution, eventually becoming one of its mainstays. Then, in 1961, two exceptional black singers made Metropolitan debuts, and both have remained with the company down to the present. One was George Shirley, a superb tenor who became the Met's finest Pelléas and Faust, among many other roles. The other was Leontyne Price, an extraordinarily pretty lyric soprano who made her debut in *Il Trovatore* opposite Franco Corelli, who was making his. Miss Price, besides being pretty, had a wonderfully warm and expressive voice of the type the Italians call *lirico spinto* (literally "pushed lyric"—a voice a bit larger and more agile than a plain lyric). She was an instant hit, and she went on to sing the role of Aida, making the most beautiful and one of the most expressive Ethiopian princesses the Met had seen in many a year. The season was an extraordinary triumph for her. Before it was over she had sung five roles (Leonora in *Il Trovatore*, Aida, Madame Butterfly, Donna Anna in Mozart's *Don Giovanni*, and Liu in Puccini's *Turandot*), and *Time* magazine had put her on its cover. Critics had raved about her perfect Verdi and Mozart voice, admired her musical style, and noted her striking appearance on the stage. She had not shown herself to be a great actress from a visual standpoint. Her presence was a bit static and uninvolved. But her voice alone was capable of bringing tears to the eyes of her listeners.

Miss Price had come to the Metropolitan well prepared. It is unusual for a singer to do five roles in her first season. But she had been familiar to audiences in New York, San Francisco, and various European (and even Asian) cities long before her Met debut, and she had sung most of those roles before. She had first come to the attention of the New York public in a small role in a revival of Virgil Thomson's opera *Four Saints in Three Acts*. (Thomson had cast her after hearing her do Mistress Ford in a student performance of *Falstaff* at the Juilliard School. Another composer, Nicholas Naboko, had heard her at the same performance, and Naboko promptly introduced her to his fellow composer Samuel Barber, who was to write a great many things especially for her, and who remained a close friend throughout her career.) *Four Saints* traveled to Paris, and Miss Price went along. A stint as Bess in a revival of Gershwin's *Porgy and Bess* followed. It opened in Dallas, was promptly sent by the State Department to Vienna, London, and other European capitals, and was finally brought to New York for a considerable run at the Ziegfeld Theatre. She then participated in an ANTA concert tour that took her as far as India. Meanwhile, André Mertens, an impresario known for his shrewdness, signed her up with the Columbia Artists Management to take advantage of her recital potentialities. One day Mertens brought her to the attention of the great Austrian conductor Herbert von Karajan, whom he persuaded to listen to her during a rehearsal break in Carnegie Hall. Von Karajan became so enthused that he jumped up onto the stage and, after a few admonitions, began to accompany her himself at the piano. The upshot was a long association with von Karajan, beginning with an appearance as Pamina in *Die Zauberflöte* under his baton at the Vienna State Opera. An engagement at La Scala followed.

Meanwhile, the then active NBC Opera, under the direction of the ex-music critic Samuel Chotzinoff and Peter Hermann Adler (now director of the NET Opera), had been presenting her as Pamina, as Donna Anna in *Don Giovanni* and also as Tosca ("A black Tosca! Can you imagine such a thing?" she had exclaimed when the idea was suggested to her). More performances in Europe with von Karajan occurred at this time, including one as Donna

139

Anna at the Salzburg Festival in 1954. And the San Francisco Opera took her on for a small role in Poulenc's *Dialogues of the Carmelites*. She soon was given the leading role of the Chief Prioress, and when Antonietta Stella, who was to have sung Aida, fell ill with appendicitis, Miss Price took over the role in her place, doing it for the first time on any stage. That season was her first on the real stage of an American opera house, and Miss Price has retained an affectionate feeling for the San Francisco Opera ever since. Kurt Herbert Adler, the able administrator of the San Francisco Opera, advised her at this point not to make her debut at the Metropolitan until she had a number of roles under her belt and not to type herself by first appearing in the black role of Aida, and she followed his advice even though the Met had begun to make approaches to her. Shortly after her San Francisco debut she sang Aida and Liu with the Chicago Lyric Opera. By 1959 she had sung Aida at Covent Garden, and the following year she sang Donna Anna again with von Karajan at the Berlin Festival. In 1960 she also sang Aida under Tullio Serafin's baton in the amphitheater at Verona before an audience of seventeen thousand people, who gave her a standing ovation.

It is not surprising, under the circumstances, that her debut at the Metropolitan was made with considerable assurance. Since then more than a decade has passed, and Miss Price has inherited nearly all the leading Verdi lyric roles that were formerly done by the great Yugoslav soprano Zinka Milanov. She has also continued her appearances in Mozart opera—an exacting field from a stylistic standpoint—and her musicianship has been termed flawless. She has repeatedly been described as the ideal Verdi lyric soprano. No rival has taken her place in the minds of operagoers. Today, though she has been singing less at the Met than formerly, she is at the peak of her career—a star whose houses are always sold out and whose autograph is pleaded for by thousands of admirers.

From the time of her Metropolitan debut, critics have been impressed by her regal bearing, as well as her voice. Her innate sense of dignity makes her an ideal impersonator of the various Spanish aristocrats Verdi was addicted to in so many of his librettos. As early as 1954, when she made a Town Hall recital debut accompanied by the eminent composer Samuel Barber, Jay Harrison, critic of the *Herald Tribune*, described her as "a goddess performing among us." Backstage she has the rather tempestuous personality that goes with dignity, plus a great fund of bubbling humor. She is sure of herself, proud of her blackness, very feminine, highly emotional and still a pretty woman, though, like all singers, she has finally put on considerable weight. Her good looks are not those of a somewhat dark white woman, as are those of Lena Horne, Barbara McNair, and others. They are those of an authentic African beauty—round-faced, round-eyed, ample-lipped, and curly-haired, with a wonderfully translucent brown skin. She claims to have some Indian blood in her veins, and there is no reason to doubt her. But she has none of the inscrutable grandeur of the Indian physiognomy. Her face is easily moved to expressions of affection, amusement, pity, or fury, and these expressions are as transparent as those of a child. As for her voice, it is a carefully controlled instrument, rich in texture, seamless throughout its range, which is roughly between A below middle C to high D, "except in the shower," she explains, where it expands in both directions. It is with this voice, rather than with bodily or facial movement, that she does most of her acting. It is magnificently attuned to the expression of emotions and moods; it is famous for its flawless legato and its melting upper register, and it can fill reaches of the Metropolitan without any signs of effort on her part. In fact, Miss Price has a principle of singing that she learned from her teacher, Florence Page Kimball, which is expressed in the words "Sing on your interest; don't use the principal." "After a performance," she confided to an interviewer, "you should be able

141

to feel that you could sing the whole thing over again without any strain."

When she is not singing or traveling somewhere to sing, Miss Price lives in an old red-brick Colonial house scarcely more than sixteen feet wide but containing thirteen rooms on Van Dam Street in Greenwich Village. The house has three inhabitants—Leontyne; a Mrs. Shoemaker, who is known as "Lulu" and serves as a housekeeper, though Leontyne always refers to her as "my friend" to remove any onus of servitude; and finally, Louella, a large German shepherd dog who is nice to acquaintances but rather savage to strangers. Louella makes a fine watchdog. The three of them are known to friends as the three L's—Leontyne, Lulu, and Louella—and they supplement each other's efforts in an important way. Lulu won't let anyone interfere in the housework, so Leontyne is well taken care of. But Lulu also fulfills another important function—that of appraising Miss Price's singing. "I'm never allowed to get too big for my britches," Miss Price remarks. "Sometimes I feel so great that I think 'Tonight I'm going to be able to wipe out a whole set of lyrics with one great tone. There's nobody who sings as gloriously as I'm going to be tonight.' And I get started singing. And then I hear Lulu from downstairs: 'Keep goin'. You're goin' to get it right! You're gettin' better. Not bad.' She sort of chops these extra airs off me. And Louella comes to the piano and helps me. She sings. She thinks she is very good at singing. She howls at fire engines, too. We're a house of stars. Everybody's a star here."

The house has an atmosphere of coziness. The front parlor, which contains a grand piano, is full of comfortable furniture, and its walls are covered with paintings that Miss Price has collected from all over the world—paintings that reveal a taste for realism or symbolism rather than abstraction. Behind this parlor and up a step or two is a small writing room where she answers her voluminous mail and keeps in touch with her family—her mother, who lives in the South, and her brother, Colonel George Price, a career Army man, now post commander at Aschaffenburg, Germany. Her social habits are modest. Occasionally a guest drops in for dinner, and she serves a dish she is famous for, called Crabmeat Imperial, which demands large portions of okra among other things. Her guests have included Roy Wilkins and other members of civil rights groups, as well as colleagues of the singing profession, managers, and so on. From time to time she goes to the Broadway theater, and she is very fond of ballet. "Actually," she confided recently, "my idea of enjoying myself in going out is *not* to go to the opera, contrary to some singers. Because I can't be completely objective. I suffer along with whoever is singing. I love the legitimate theater"—and with an air of surprised discovery— "the story line is expressed without sung sound, and it just fascinates me! I'm also crazy about ballet. It's the most beautiful art form to watch. I like the Royal Ballet, Fonteyn and Nureyev. I'm also an Erik Bruhn fan, and I love to go to the Balanchine ballet. I also like the Alvin Ailey company. He's a good friend of mine. He's done so many wonderful things. He has a black prima donna who is marvelous—like a swan." Has she any favorite Broadway actors or actresses? "It fluctuates. One year my favorite actress was Lauren Bacall, because I thought she was, as they say, out of sight. The next it was Alexis Smith in *Follies*. I also go to the movies quite a bit, and I like anything that has to do with history— *Nicholas and Alexandra* for example. I don't look at television much. It interferes with my reading. But I like Flip Wilson and Carol Burnett—two of the most intelligent and fascinating people in the world. I've been able to become part of the New York community," she continued with obvious pleasure. "I like to enjoy all the wonderful things New York has to present." All this is spoken in Northern English with only an occasional hint of a Southern drawl. When Miss Price is not engaged in concert tours or out-of-town opera appearances, she is very much a city woman, and her favorite city, despite her familiarity with many others, is New York.

The house, with its air of coziness, is a refuge where Miss Price can turn the outer world off and be with her own thoughts, and she is one of those people who have to turn the outer world off in order to reach a sense of security. She worries about her operatic roles and is not too enthusiastic about putting herself on display. Each performance at the opera house has its terrors for her. She usually eats a steak at home at about four o'clock in the afternoon before an appearance, and has another one after it is over. She gets so keyed up at a performance that she cannot sleep that night at all, and so spends the night rethinking what she did, writing letters, reading, and so on. This insomnia is so habitual that she does not even attempt to go to bed, just sits up and thinks all night. "I usually allow two days to unwind after a performance. I do crazy things, even cleaning up, straightening up my closets, anything to take my mind off what I have been doing on the stage," she remarks. Unlike the easygoing, exhibitionistic figure people imagine opera singers to be, Miss Price is extraordinarily nervous and sensitive about her work. She never allows seats on the stage to be sold for her recitals. "Maybe it's a sort of claustrophobia," she once said. "I don't have enough room. I can't stand having people behind me. I don't like roomettes in trains. It's that kind of thing. Besides, if somebody on the stage coughs or rattles a program, I just feel I'd like them to go away. I don't think I'm alone in that." According to her coach, Otto Guth, she often gets overinvolved in her roles. She has been known to weep on the stage during performances of *Madame Butterfly*, and each appearance she makes is a fresh challenge to be overcome. Despite her enormous success, there remains in her mind a certain incredulity, and a certain feeling of unease about being a Southern black girl who has climbed into the international limelight.

The success itself is demonstrable on every hand. She insists on, and gets, the highest fee paid at any opera house where she sings, and her annual income is measured in six figures. She is a celebrated figure in London, Paris, Milan, Vienna, and Rome, as well as in Hamburg, where she expects to do a good deal of singing in the near future. Her fans are as articulate as those of any diva. Two white college boys from Shreveport, Louisiana, became so enthused about her that they brought flowers to her dressing room after a New Orleans concert, and were somewhat abashed to meet her personally (they had expected just to leave the flowers and go). Later they followed her by bus to Bloomington, Indiana, and then all the way to San Francisco. "If Miss Price can get out of the South, so can we," they said proudly to the other standees at the San Francisco Opera. After one performance there, they brought her a mechanical toy they had made—a woodcut scene from *Il Trovatore* in which Leonora is being stabbed by the Count di Luna. It has a crank which, when turned, makes the dagger go in and out of Leonora's chest. Miss Price still keeps it in her writing room. There is another young man (also white) who works for British European Airways and who gets a pass to fly to New York whenever she sings. In a reverse way, even Mr. Bing ("He has always treated me with respect," she notes) paid her a similar compliment by getting furious when he discovered that she had a photograph of Von Karajan on her dressing table at the Met. Why didn't she have a photograph of *him*? She soon repaired the oversight, and Mr. Bing was placated.

When Miss Price first arrived in New York from the South, she had no idea what an opera was. Her first experience with the art form came when she attended a performance of *Salome* at the Met in which Ljuba Welitsch was singing the title role. She decided then and there to become a professional opera singer, and she became a friend of Miss Welitsch, whom she still visits every time she goes to Vienna. This was while Miss Price was still a student at the Juilliard School, studying with Florence Page Kimball, an ex-singer who helped develop her voice and who has remained a lifelong friend whom Miss Price consults before making a move. Even today, she goes to Miss Kimball for a vocal lesson once a week whenever she is in New York, and Miss Kimball has gone to Europe with her several times to help keep her voice in shape and to watch proudly while her pupil has caused a sensation in one capital or another. Her loyalty to Miss Kimball is exceeded only by her loyalty to her family—her mother, who lives in the South, her brother, George, and George's four children. "He is the family's progenitor," she explains.

Miss Price was married at one time to the baritone William Warfield, who was the Porgy in the *Porgy and Bess* production with which she traveled. The marriage didn't work out. Because of their conflicting careers, they seldom saw each other, and finally they got a legal separation. Miss Price, however, has no desire to remarry, and she is the best of friends with Warfield, who goes to hear her performances and sometimes advises her. The house in Van Dam Street was purchased, in fact, while they were married, and when they separated, Warfield amicably moved out, leaving Mrs. Shoemaker, who had been his housekeeper previously. But Miss Price is very fond of masculine company. When she appeared in *Dialogues of the Carmelites* in San Francisco (the cast is made up exclusively of nuns), the director, Harry Horner, a very earnest man, suggested that they live like nuns while the opera was being rehearsed. "There were thirteen or fifteen women in the cast," she explains. "We were all very kind to each other. We ate our hamburgers very quietly together. It was a very unhealthy atmosphere. There wasn't a single fella, and we were thrown together with each other. It was pretty drastic. It was the nearest I'll ever get to a convent. There's no doubt about that. I couldn't help thinking the next role I would like to sing would be *La Traviata*."

When Antonietta Stella had her appendectomy and Miss Price

took over the role of Aida in her place, the nervous, energetic costumer of the San Francisco Opera—a woman named Rose Goldstein—suggested that she appear in dark blue in the first act and in dark brown in the second. Miss Price objected. She wanted brighter colors. "But," said Miss Goldstein, "they should be dark, because you have to clean them after every performance to get all that dark body makeup off." "I've got that dark body makeup built in," Miss Price said, and Miss Goldstein for the first time realized that she was dealing with a black singer. Miss Price often jokes about her color. Once, at a coaching session with Mr. Guth, she was having trouble getting a phrase right. After trying it over and over again, she finally said, "Let's face it; we haven't all got rhythm." Mr. Guth once remarked, "She arrives here radiant, exploding with laughter. Sometimes the phone rings while we are at work, and since I am seated at the piano, it is usually the singer who answers it. Most of them stop singing and answer the phone. Not Leontyne. She takes up the receiver and finishes the phrase she is singing, giving the caller a taste of her voice. *Then* she says, 'Just a minute.' She always puts the phone back correctly. She is very meticulous about her behavior. She writes me letters from wherever she is. Some singers just use me, but not Leontyne. She's a good friend." Guth also confirms what many people, including Harriet Johnson, music critic of the New York *Post* and an expert on voices, have said, that Miss Price has a natural aptitude for languages and that her diction in French and German, as well as Italian, is practically perfect. Mr. Warfield notes that her German is spoken with a slight Viennese accent because she has been in Vienna so many times. The talent is apparently one for mimicry. When *Porgy and Bess* was in London, Warfield remembers, Miss Price adopted a "veddy veddy" British accent and used it at an embassy party, causing some raised eyebrows, as well as great amusement on the part of those who knew her well. Mr. Guth is only one of the four people "who manage to get me onstage," as she

147

modestly explains it. Like all opera singers, as well as those who specialize in concerts, she has to have a coach to listen to her singing as outsiders hear it and to touch up certain points of phrasing and pronunciation. Mr. Guth is her New York coach. She has another one in Europe—a certain Maestro Luigi Ricci who lives in Rome. And then there is her accompanist, David Garvey, a black pianist who has been with her since Juilliard days ("He studied at Juilliard at the same time I did, and I think he's the world's greatest pianist. We've known each other for twenty years, and he has toured with me often"). And finally there is the indispensable Miss Kimball. "Between Mr. Guth and Maestro Ricci, I have had all the operatic parts I know drummed into my head. Miss Kimball takes care of my voice, and David Garvey appears with me in concerts and is a big help, too."

Miss Price has had a couple of terrible crises in her career at the Metropolitan. The first of them was the result of not heeding Miss Kimball's advice about "singing on the interest and leaving the principal untouched." Six or seven years ago, she was singing the role of Minnie in Puccini's *Fanciulla del West* at the Metropolitan. She became overambitious, and sang Beethoven's "Ach du Abscheulicher" from *Fidelio*, a rather strenuous aria, with von Karajan at a concert in Carnegie Hall between two *Fanciullas*. At the second *Fanciulla* she broke down in the second act. Her voice simply cracked, and she couldn't go on. Dorothy Kirsten was called on short notice to substitute for her during the rest of the opera. According to Francis Robinson, the Met's public relations man, historian, and assistant director, the great soprano of yesteryear, Rosa Raisa, was in the audience that night, and Miss Price knew it. She was crushed with humiliation, cried all the way home in a taxi with Marcia Davenport and George Marek, then head of RCA Victor Records, and did not rebound completely for a couple of seasons afterward. "It was a real crisis for her," Guth explains. "Leontyne is often scared, though she doesn't show it. All singers start an evening badly. The trick is to disguise it so that it is not obvious. Later they get better. Warming up beforehand doesn't help because there's no audience to be frightened of. And every time you have to prove that you are bigger than life."

But Miss Price did recover her confidence completely and went on to achieve the finest moments of her career. It was just at this peak that the Metropolitan opened its new house in Lincoln Center, and Miss Price was chosen for the opening night as the star of Samuel Barber's *Anthony and Cleopatra*, a great honor for any singer. The designer of the sets and costumes, as well as the director of the production, was the famous Italian theater man Franco Zeffirelli. The performance was more or less of a disaster. Mr. Zeffirelli had overstaged the opera to the point where Barber's music was scarcely noticeable, though it was music of sterling qualities and probably would have survived a more modest production. But these flaws, which were universally noted by the critics, were nothing compared to the personal experiences of Miss Price in the role of Cleopatra. "If Sam Barber was discouraged, I was devastated," she recalls. "I could write a book. I don't think that anybody else, and I say it immodestly, would have stood what I stood to open that house. It was beyond endurance. It was the greatest honor for any living singer. But I didn't feel that I would get out of it with my life. I was never so reminded that I was black as I was during this particular responsibility. I don't know whether anybody knows about this, but there were crank calls, anonymous letters, threats of bombing the house. To be an artist, you have to take the responsibility of performing as best you can. This is a great responsibility, believe me. To know that if you catch a common cold, it could actually become an international event in musical circles—which meant a whole year of never sitting in drafts or doing anything that might even bring on a small sneeze. I find it difficult to talk about. The thing was a traumatic experience partly because I alone was being given this plum, and there must have

149

Leontyne Price as a young girl of sixteen.

Leontyne Price with her family and fans backstage, after the opening night of the new Metropolitan Opera house in September, 1966. The opera was Samuel Barber's *Anthony and Cleopatra*. Standing left to right are her father, James A. Price; her brother, Colonel George B. Price; and her mother, Kate Baker Price.

The NY Times

Leontyne Price first performed the title role of Puccini's *Madame Butterfly* in Vienna in 1960.

Photograph by Hubert Dilworth

As Aida in Verdi's opera.

Photograph by Anthony Crickmay

Leontyne Price as Amelia in Verdi's *Un Ballo in Maschera* at the San Francisco Opera.

Leontyne Price as Elvira in Verdi's *Ernani*.

been other American singers who said, 'Why her, and not me?' That's human nature. All singers think they sing better than the next person anyway, and that's all right. But if you were an opera singer, to open a new house? I wouldn't recommend it. The pressure of the responsibility of the opening itself, and the fact that Sam Barber had recommended me for the role, why, it got on my nerves. I earned every bit of the honor of opening that house by virtue of my talent and my work, my personal work as an artist. I did not feel that anybody had given me a great gift. I did not want to disappoint *myself*; that was the main thing. My work was done with the hard work and sacrifices of so many people. That was what was at stake. To people in the music business it was a plum, and it *was* really. It was the kind of exposure movie stars dream about. But I really paid for the responsibility and the honor. Paid in full."

Part of the trouble was the overelaborate scenery Zeffirelli had designed, with a moving sphinx as big as a locomotive which was supposed to be hauled around by the Metropolitan's new turntable. During the rehearsals the turntable broke down, not to be repaired for years afterward, and Mr. Zeffirelli's sphinx had to be moved by a group of stagehands walking inside it. Besides all this, Miss Price was given a sphinxlike costume and headdress that made her look more like Aunt Jemima than Cleopatra. "Ten days before the performance," Miss Price remembered, "everything was chaotic. Nothing was right. The one good thing was the beautiful music that Sam wrote, music which was written with my voice in mind. That's why it fit so well. But every day there was something different. They changed costumes continually. I only remember losing my temper once at the Metropolitan, and that was during these rehearsals. Everything could be solved by congenial means, I thought. Since I was on the spot, I tried to conduct myself in a controlled way. But I left one rehearsal, and I went to Mr. Bing, and I said that there were many things I would do to open the

Metropolitan—but that they didn't include either my soul or my life. Peace of mind was out the window. One specific problem was moving into a new house, with all the technical things like whether the stage was going to work or not. They should have been tried out before. That was what created the original chaos. I thought I was going to end up in a rest home somewhere. We had three weeks of rehearsal, but catastrophes happened at every performance. There was never a smooth one."

Zeffirelli's scenic arrangements turned out to be a nightmare for everybody. He had put a golden pyramid in the center of the stage, and Miss Price was supposed to emerge from it and then go to the side of the stage to put on her "blue number" for the rest of the act, "and zip it up." "Well, in the first place, I couldn't get out of the pyramid. There I am, looking for a way out. Let's face it. It was a frantic thing. Finally, they pulled the thing back far enough for me to crawl out, which wasn't easy with all that fabric. I heard Maestro Schippers playing the music, and I had to come out. I came out with only half of that darned thing pulled together. The costume was two-thirds on; I hadn't been able to get out of it. I had nothin' else to put on. The 'blue number' was out of the question. I had to play the rest of the act in that same costume. It was scary. It may seem funny now, but it wasn't funny at all. I refuse to go mad. But it was just so chaotic that I thought, 'Well, I'll just try to sing.' There was devastating chaos all around. And there was no improvement in the performances that followed. Something was always wrong."

The experience gave her a permanent dislike for Zeffirelli, and she vowed never to sing in one of his productions again. On the other hand, she has insisted—like any top prima donna—on a new production from time to time. "It's not exactly a thrill to go up to Sixty-third street and do the same old Aida," she remarked the other day. "Why shouldn't I have a new pair of pants?" A couple of years ago, Mr. Bing decided to give her a new production of *Il*

155

Trovatore. She was delighted until she heard that Mr. Bing wanted Zeffirelli to design and direct the production. She put her foot down. She would not sing under those circumstances. So Mr. Bing fell back on Attillio Colonello, whose designs were even worse than Zeffirelli's. Miss Price dutifully sang in this production, but she was getting fed up with Mr. Bing's designers. The following season she didn't sing at the Met at all. "Mr. Bing was livid with anger when I told him I was not going to sing that season, but that was that. I had made up my mind." The season after that she sang four performances of *La Forza del Destino*, and that was all. Meanwhile, she had sung for two solid months at the San Francisco Opera. "After all, that's where I made my debut," she explained.

Miss Price's loyalties are fierce and lasting. Her loyalty to her ex-husband in spite of their separation is remarkable. Her loyalty to Miss Kimball, whom she refers to as "Mary" or "Teacher," is unbounded, and she consults her on practically every move she makes. She is also extremely loyal to her family. Recently her mother had an accident in which she broke her hip, and was laid up in the hospital for a long period. Leontyne flew to Mississippi to see her every weekend and sometimes in between. A bout of flu followed the operation on her hip, and Leontyne was told by the doctor to keep her alert. So Leontyne stayed up night after night, talking rapidly to her mother except during those periods when sleep was inevitable. "Stay awake, Momma," she kept saying, and then she had an idea. There were two friends of the family at the bedside. "Momma, who is that standing on the left side of the bed?" she asked. "That's Charlotte, my godchild," her mother replied. "And who is that at the foot of the bed?" "Oh, that's Isabella." "And who am I?" "Oh, you're Madame Butterfly." Her mother's convalescence lasted a long time, and Leontyne was at her bedside every time she could get away from her concert and opera schedule.

Several years ago, Von Karajan persuaded Miss Price, against her better judgment, to record a performance of *Carmen*. Miss Price, who has never sung Carmen on the stage, thought of the event as a sort of joke, anyhow as a lark. "I did it with Corelli, Freni, and Merrill," she recalls. "It never occurred to me that it was some great thing. I was extremely naïve for a long time. You know, if somebody educates you and says, 'That was a very difficult high C,' you can't sing it anymore. That was the theory on which I recorded *Carmen*. I never had so much fun in my life. And I hadn't the slightest interest in doing *Carmen*. *He* [Von Karajan] had the idea in mind; no doubt about that. And, of course, he is a fantastic vocal conductor. I was invited by him to do a new production of *Carmen* in Salzburg, but I refused. I don't have an interest in doing it. Oh, I think Carmen is a fantastic character. Definitely. But I don't think she's terribly rewarding. She never has all the stage to herself like we do in Verdi. Just to be hypertechnical about it, I think Carmen works much too hard for the check she gets in the end. It's really hard work. I look at Carmen like I look at Butterfly, which I would like to do again one of these days. I could do three Aidas to one Butterfly. Butterfly is never by herself. It's really a day's work. She has to keep house and lift children, clean up the place. I think histrionically they're marvelous parts, but if you analyze them vocally, they're not as rewarding as Leonora in *Trovatore,* I mean really putting a miscroscope to them. But as just something to get my teeth into, it's really a waste of time for me to do Carmen onstage." Nevertheless, the *Carmen* recording has sold widely, and has added a great deal to her mounting accumulation of record royalties. As the above quotation shows, Miss Price is more interested in singing than in acting from a visual standpoint, and in the recording studio she is free of all the visual business that has to take place on the stage. "I think," she muses, "that recording is in a way much more personal than stage performance. In a theater the audience sees and hears you. So the costumes and general *mise en scène* help you do the job, because they can see. In recording, you have to see and hear for them with the voice—which makes it much more personal."

Miss Price, among other things, is a very religious woman. "I don't like discussions about my religion," she once said. "My belief in God is very childlike—terribly uncomplicated. I don't like to tamper with it. I believe firmly that everything that has happened to me is caused by God. I don't like this touched by anyone. I do know that He is there, and if He wasn't, I don't know where I would be. I go to church in New York less than I used to. I still consider myself a member of the so-called Methodist Church. I go to church much more often at home. One of my favorite churches in New York is the Fifth Avenue Presbyterian Church. They have a man named Dr. Kirkland. He always gives me something to start the week with. Besides, their vesper services are so warm. But I am really a member of the Washington Square Methodist Church."

At a fortieth anniversary dinner, given by *Time* magazine several years ago for all the people who had appeared on its cover, Miss Price found herself seated alongside Francis Cardinal Spellman, and on the other side of him sat Clare Boothe Luce. Miss Price's job was to sing the national anthem. The cardinal and Mrs. Luce fell into a discussion as to how many of those present were Catholics. Finally, the cardinal turned to Miss Price and asked, "My daughter, are you a Catholic?" "No, *Eminenza*," replied Miss Price ingenuously, "I am a Methodist." The cardinal was slightly taken aback, but he liked the title *Eminenza*. Later on in Rome, where Miss Price has a flat in the rather ecclesiastical neighborhood of Hadrian's tomb, the cardinal called her and invited her to lunch. Miss Price was very wary. She said, "First I've got to know why?" The cardinal reassured her that no proselytizing purpose was involved, and the lunch went by in a friendly atmosphere.

Miss Price takes her Christian charity very seriously. She has sung countless benefits for the Southern Christian Leadership Conference (both Roy Wilkins and Martin Luther King were close friends), and she has given considerable sums to Dorothy Maynor's Harlem School of the Arts—all without any publicity—along with gifts to her hometown church and the Ohio college from which she graduated. At one point she brought a bedridden girl in an ambulance all the way from Forty Fort, Pennsylvania, to the Metropolitan to hear her sing in *La Forza del Destino*. She has also helped young singers, including prominently Veronica Tyler and Joyce Mathis. In doing so, she has been reported to say, "Come on over, dear, we've got to get together. There's only so many high C's left in the old diva." Her generosity is legendary. So is her temper, which sometimes flares over a small slight of some sort. She is capable of denouncing somebody—sometimes another singer, sometimes a manager like Mr. Bing—in ringing tones. Then, afterward, she invariably goes into a mood of self-hatred and remorse, saying, "How could I have said that?" Opera houses are remarkable for fostering these small tempests. Mr. Guth remarks, "Relations between singers and impresarios of opera houses are always strained. They really don't like each other. They act like sulky children. This is because the impresario is primarily concerned with getting the show on the road, regardless of the strain that might be involved for any particular artist. Often the artist feels that he has been singing too much, or that he would prefer not to sing a certain role in the shape his voice is in. And the manager overrules him. That doesn't make for absolutely smooth relationships."

There are many explanations of why Miss Price is not singing so much today in opera as she used to. Guth says that there is a paranoid atmosphere about most opera houses, and an enormous sense of competitiveness, neither of which appeals to Miss Price. Warfield maintains that though opera was once a great challenge to her, it is no longer so, and that she is now more challenged by the

159

field of recitals. As for Miss Price herself, she has a totally different explanation. "I feel," she says, "that you have to rest the voice and avoid pressure for considerable periods. You have to reflect, too. I've been singing less and less everywhere. You cannot keep up that kind of pressure. I'm asked to be booked more and more, but look, I'd like to find out who I am. If I do have some success, I'd like to try to enjoy it, for heaven's sake! What is the point of having it otherwise? Everybody else gets excited, but *you're* the one who's always tired. That's not life; that's not living. Also, if you keep it up indefinitely, I don't think you perform as well. I think you have to have time to learn new materials. I think a career, if it is good, should be handled like something really beautiful. You know, it's really a love affair with the public acceptance of you. And you cannot do that if you do not have some time to give to something new, even some time to breathe. You need time to study more, to learn new things, to improve things in the voice that you know require correction, things that you might have been able to do naturally five years ago but that need a little more work. Also, you should get out and see people more. There are people, you know, who don't think the whole day begins and ends with opera. There are even people who don't have the slightest idea what an opera singer is. I have a very personal reason for not singing so much. It's just Leontyne trying to find out about Leontyne. I'm beginning to forget what I started out with—the completely natural joy of singing. It's almost coming back, and I'm trying not to lose it. I've begun to go to the theater. I've even begun to sit in drafts, which I think is the greatest gift of all—to sit in an air-conditioned room without cracking up. I've begun to enjoy life."

As Warfield says, "She's not basically a traveler. The idea of getting on and off planes is something she doesn't cotton to." And though she does necessarily travel a good deal, she stays a long time in each place she visits. In general, she sings about one concert a week and then, like most divas, spends the summer recording. The

cities she sings in in this country are what she calls "open" cities—
cities where black people can expect to be treated with respect—
and she mentions New Orleans and Miami in this connection. For
some reason, she has never agreed to sing in Memphis. Apparently
it is on her blacklist. On the Metropolitan's 1964 spring tour, she
sang in Atlanta, but refused to sing in Dallas, where she felt that
Kennedy's blood was still on the ground. Only after Mr. Bing had
called her attention to the fact that she had often sung in Vienna,
where many people were carried off to concentration camps, did
she agree to sing there. Her political involvements are intense and
varied, but before getting to them, we ought to consider her origins
and background.

There are five characters in the story of her life who were crucial
to her development, and they all live, or lived, in the little
Mississippi town of Laurel, where she was born and named Mary
Violet Leontyne Price. Three of these were her mother, Mrs.
Katherine Price, a strong, proud woman standing a few inches
taller than Miss Price herself, who taught her the art of getting
along in a white-dominated world and who, in later life, became a
midwife and pillar of Laurel's black community; her father, Mr.
James Anthony Price, a quiet, reflective man who earned a living
as a carpenter, and a favorite aunt, known to the family as "Big
Auntie," who followed Leontyne's development with avid interest
and who worked as a maid in the home of a white couple known as
the Chisholms. These first three lived on South Fifth Avenue, a dirt
road that ran as far as Magnolia Street, where it suddenly changes
into North Fifth Avenue, a paved street where Laurel's white
families live. The Alexander Chisholms lived on North Fifth
Avenue. Mr. Chisholm is a Northerner from Vermont who had
made a lot of money in Laurel, in lumber, in oil, and, finally, in
banking. He is Laurel's top dog, and he and his wife often help
Laurel's younger people, both black and white, to get on in life.
The Chisholms were, and still are, people of excellent intentions,

and the time came when they were of assistance to Leontyne. But a myth, which might be called the "Chisholm legend," grew, largely because it made good newspaper copy, that the white Chisholms were responsible for the career of the black girl Leontyne, and this has distressed both Leontyne and the Chisholms. The fact of the matter is that Leontyne's father and mother worked hard and mortgaged their home in order to send Leontyne and her brother, George, to college, and that they saw to Leontyne's early musical training. "I had musical palpitations ever since I was four," Miss Price explains, "and everybody, especially Big Auntie, thought I was some kind of a musical prodigy." She studied the piano with Hattie V. J. McKenna, a local teacher, and before long, she was playing both the organ and the piano in Laurel's black Methodist church. She is still a pretty good pianist, and studies her roles at the piano, as well as plays occasionally for friends. The Price family was very close. "I did not know I was poor," she remembers. "My family was affluent in love, deep religious background, respect for our fellowman, affection, faith, and simplicity—a hell of a combination. My mother is such a part of the community that even now, when she is not particularly well, she is still available to every problem. There are teen-agers who come to her. She is constantly a service to her community." Mrs. Katherine Price is an educated woman. She attended Rusk College at Holly Springs, just outside Memphis, when it was just a one-building campus for blacks, and she was insistent that her daughter get an even better education. So Leontyne went to Central State College at Wilberforce, Ohio, which was then a black school, and, on graduation, got a certificate entitling her to teach music in the public schools. Her ambitions were already beyond that, but it was something to fall back on in case of need.

What first stimulated these ambitions was a concert given by Marian Anderson in Jackson, where her mother took her when she was a little girl. "I was nine and a half," Miss Price remembers, "when I first heard Marian Anderson. It was just a vision of elegance and nobility. It was one of the most enthralling, marvelous experiences I've ever had. I can't tell you how inspired I was to do something even similar to what she was doing. That was what you might call the original kickoff. "Later, at Central State College, she had another experience of the sort. Central State is close to Antioch College, and the choirs of the two colleges often got together to sing oratorios like Handel's *The Messiah*. Paul Robeson, the great black baritone, visited Antioch to do some lecturing and singing, and at his recital there he invited Leontyne to sing part of the program and gave her half the receipts. She saved this money, and augmented it by working in the college cafeteria. On graduation, she made straight for New York, where she got a scholarship at the Juilliard School and meanwhile worked behind the information desk at International House, where she lived. Miss Kimball, then a teacher at Juilliard, took her under her wing. It was at this time that the Chisholms began to help her in her career, though they had also helped her get to New York. And they remained devoted friends. There was, however, the presence of the "Chisholm legend," which eventually drove Leontyne into a rebellious frame of mine. "Everything that has a bearing on my career," she says with some bitterness, "has *not* necessarily to do with the Chisholms. A lot of publicity came along, because it was chic to think that a white family in deep Mississippi had helped a black girl become a success, and the newspapers made the most of it. Although they helped me a great deal, I worked in their home as a maid during my spare time for extra money during the summer holidays in between the years in college. My aunt was their domestic servant for quite a number of years, and I used to sing in their home for parties and different functions, and when it was time to go away, they helped me. It's not true that they paid for my college education. My father and mother paid for my college work and also helped me when I was in school. This is something that I

163

want to correct. I think some literature ought to be written on how it feels to be a token black—which I was. Perhaps I will write some of it. Any time that anybody could point to a token black, we were represented as people's conscience, to allay their feeling of guilt. There was much more attention paid to this particular white-black relationship, because it was of news value, than to these two marvelous people, my father and mother, who were responsible for my career. It was not chic to mention that my father and mother were alive. This is one of the most devastating things about being a token black, and it is something all token blacks have had to go through. It has hit me especially in this time of my life when I have had time to reflect. The Chisholms are still alive, but I don't want to hurt my parents. I have felt bad about this. All token blacks have the same experience. I have been pointed at as a solution to things that have not *begun* to be solved, because pointing at us token blacks eases the conscience of millions, and I think this is dreadfully wrong."

As a Southern black, Leontyne was taught to keep her mouth shut about white-black relations, and even when she came to New York, she had to, as she expresses it, "walk on my tippy toes," for fear of rousing resentment. Her situation in this matter represents in capsule form the whole struggle for pride among America's blacks. They do not want to be given things and say thank you. They want to achieve things on their own and get credit for doing so. Miss Price is very definite in her opinions about this problem, even going so far as to back, in thought at least, the Black Panthers and other militant black groups. "When I first appeared, I couldn't be outspoken. When people like Whitney Young and Martin Luther King were said to be not outspoken enough, I'm in great company. I was part of the black liberation movement by virtue of the fact that I was a token black. When white people say, 'Look, isn't it great that we have a black singer?' that's their problem, not mine."

Both Whitney Young and Martin Luther King were close personal friends of Miss Price, and when the latter was assassinated, she felt the blow as if it had been intended for her. When Medgar Evers was killed, close to her home territory in Mississippi, she underwent an outward transformation. She adopted an Afro hairdo (except on the stage) and began to speak out in no uncertain terms. "I am involved in my own way," she remarks. "One must live one's own way—that is what we fight for, to be a complete human being, an individual. That's what freedom is supposed to be. I cannot set myself up as a prefabricated example because of a bit of applause. I'm not removed from it any more than a person in a small community is. I am in an art form which is not part of anything, because it is regarded as bourgeois, Establishment entertainment. But I have always demanded things. I have never been a musical patsy for anybody. No one who has dealt with me has dared not to treat me with respect. Whether they like me or not doesn't concern me; but I insist that they respect me. As for the young militant blacks, they have made it a lot easier for the rest of us." Miss Price is passionately devoted to the black liberation movement, and has been for some time. She sends money to fighters in its cause, and she sings benefits for nearly all the most prominent organizations that specialize in furthering black independence and advance. White friends—and she has many of them—were somewhat taken aback when she made that outward transformation after the murder of Medgar Evers, but Leontyne was that way inside long before that murder took place. She was just walking on her "tippy toes."

When rapid travel between New York and Laurel became difficult, and she had trouble reaching her sick mother (there is no direct plane. On commercial transportation you must fly to New Orleans and then spend two and a half hours driving), the Chisholms offered her the use of their private plane, and she was really grateful. The Chisholms, who are proud of anything they might have done to help along a person who is now a great figure in the operatic world, often come to New York to hear her sing at the Met. And her relations with the white world are generally generous and kindly.

She has a sure sense of what roles are appropriate for her voice. Mr. Bing once offered her the heavy dramatic role of Abigaille in Verdi's *Nabucco*. Her answer was simply, "Mr. Bing, are you crazy?" And when an interviewer recently asked her whether she would ever sing Lady Macbeth in Verdi's opera *Macbeth*, she said with a smile, "I think my voice is just too beautiful to waste on a role like that" (actually, Lady Macbeth is sung only by a very special type of singer—a dramatic soprano with a certain amount of fioritura). And though the role of Donna Anna, which she has sung many times, is a fairly florid one, she admits, "Coloratura technique is not really my *pièce de résistance*. But as an extra bonus, I'm working on it. You should have fioritura. In the last few years I've worked on my coloratura a lot. It's been lots of fun." Onstage, Miss Price always seems utterly at ease. But this appearance is deceptive. "It's been only for a couple of years," she remarks, "that I have finally been able to go onstage without having added to me my thought 'This is the Metropolitan.' It's a terrible thought. I guess I got rid of it when I began to realize that you can make a mistake and not feel that the whole earth is going to fall apart. I think that is probably the most wonderful experience that I'm having now, because for so long, being a token black, you never felt mentally, emotionally, that your feet hit the bottom of anything. You were always on a tightrope. If there was one slip, you didn't fall yourself; a lot of people fell with you. So you were always *on,* shall we say. You see, it is already enough to be *on,* just to get onto the stage, but you add to it what I call extra monkeys on your back. As the kids say, it's a little heavy."

With the possible exceptions of William Faulkner and Eudora

Welty, Miss Price is Mississippi's greatest cultural gift to American civilization. And though she may agonize occasionally over the problem of civil liberties, she is regarded everywhere as an extraordinary artist. There are moments when she comes under the glare of a captious critical eye. She herself tells a story about waiting in a receiving line after a recital. "There was a gentleman there. His face was radiant. I was sure he was the sort of person who really enjoys your singing. And so I was just talking to people and waiting with great anticipation to touch him. I put out both arms, waiting for a great compliment. And, with a smile on his face, he said, 'Oh, Miss Price, I can't tell you how wonderful it is to meet you.' I said, 'I can't tell you how wonderful it is to have you.' I thought he was going to say, 'How on earth do you sing so magnificently?' Instead, he said, 'I would like to know if you felt, as I did, that there was a slight strain on your B-flat this evening?' Everything fell flat. I looked at him sternly and said, 'Sir, I have never detected any strain on my B-flat. Thanks a lot.' "

On the whole, she is optimistic about the progress that is being made toward integration. There is a restaurant in Laurel called the Magnolia Tree. Often, as a little girl, she looked wistfully at the place, which was open only to whites. But not long ago the minister of her church took her there for dinner. She looked at the bill of fare. "I was so impressed," she remembered. "Maybe integration was sort of movin' along. This was my community. I was so elated, so happy. The third item on the bill of fare was 'wop salad, special today.' I was so furious that such a thing could happen." Could it be that people in Laurel were as prejudiced against Italians as they were against blacks? "Mississippi is a closed society," Miss Price replied. "Let's face it, it's the original closed society."

Photograph by Bender N.Y.

Miss Farrell as Medea in Cherubini's *Medea*.

VI
Eileen Farrell

The inclusion of Eileen Farrell here requires some explanation. She is unquestionably one of the greatest dramatic sopranos alive today. On the other hand, owing to a number of factors that will presently become apparent, her operatic career has been an intermittent affair. A great part of the international operatic audience has never heard of her, and most of her operatic singing, though fervently admired by the few who have heard her, has been in roles that were not ideal for her. She was hired by the Metropolitan in 1960 and was unceremoniously dropped from its roster in 1965 when the Met moved into its new quarters at Lincoln Center. She disliked Mr. Bing, who happened to be running the opera house, and Mr. Bing disliked her. She is a woman of very outspoken habits and made no secrets of her likes and dislikes. If Mr. Bing had been canny enough to roll with the punches and encourage her in spite of them, he might have had an Isolde and a Brünnhilde at least equal to those of Birgit Nilsson. But Mr. Bing never made a secret of the fact that he disliked Wagnerian opera, and, at the time Miss Farrell was at the Met, the most important Wagnerian operas—the *Ring* and *Tristan und Isolde*—were not being done there. Miss Farrell was asked to sing in *La Gioconda*,

Alceste, La Forza del Destino, Andrea Chénier, and *Cavalleria Rusticana*—roles that were easy enough for her, but roles that made no demands on her formidable abilities. When her contract failed to be renewed in 1965, she shrugged her shoulders and pretty much disappeared from the operatic scene. She had never had the passionate devotion to a career that inspires most divas. She was happier as a housewife. From then on, she contented herself with an occasional recital, with remunerative appearances on television, and with collecting royalties on her numerous popular records. Yet the memories of her successful appearances are still treasured by many operagoers.

These appearances date from a concert performance of Luigi Cherubini's *Medea* in Town Hall on the evening of November 8, 1955. As a result of this performance, the small world inhabited by music critics and dedicated connoisseurs of opera underwent a distinct tremor. It was a pleasant tremor, such as might attend the winning of the Kentucky Derby by a dark horse who had never won a race before, for in the operatic field Miss Farrell was a dark horse indeed. She was a newcomer to opera on the concert platform, to say nothing of the opera house, and when she came onstage, she took up her position behind a music stand, prepared to refresh her memory by turning the pages of a score—a practice ordinarily frowned upon by the fastidious directors of the American Opera Society, the valiant, pathbreaking, and at that time fashionable organization that had sponsored the concert. This was a special concession, obviously, and it underlined the fact that Miss Farrell was then, at thirty-five, noted primarily as a radio singer— a profession where scores could be freely used. As she stood there with her eye on the score, she displayed, in the phrase of one observer, as much animation as a totem pole, and this stolidity, together with her rather bulky figure, suggested that she was not likely ever to join the ranks of prima donnas noted for their acting ability, as well as for their voices. Still, operagoers whose memories reached as far back as Luisa Tetrazzini and Margarete

Matzenauer reflected that in the so-called golden age of opera bulk had often been associated with great singing. And as soon as Miss Farrell opened her mouth, there was no denying that her singing was great by any standards. She cast over her audience the peculiar spell that, for voice enthusiasts, blots out visual experience in the sheer joy of song.

If Miss Farrell's appearance raised some doubts about whether she could act for the eye, there was not the slightest question but that she was a consummate actress for the ear. Through her voice, Cherubini's Greek heroine—a tragically maddened woman who murders her own children—emerged with the most convincing theatrical realism and with an astonishing intensity of feeling. Miss Farrell's voice seemed limitless in power, magnificent in tone, remarkably sure in its command of classical style, and accurate enough to cope successfully with any of the taxing coloratura phrases that occur so frequently in *Medea* and other Italian operas of the late eighteenth and early nineteenth centuries. Inevitably, in the days that followed the performance, comparisons with better-known opera singers were drawn, since comparisons are part of the ritual observed by every entrapped opera buff. Just at that time, indeed, an unofficial contest that was widely publicized as "the battle of the sopranos" was going on, the favored gladiators being Renata Tebaldi, Zinka Milanov, and Maria Meneghini Callas. The contest was pretty silly, as most experienced operagoers knew. Miss Tebaldi and Miss Milanov might conceivably have been considered rivals, but Miss Callas was an altogether different type of singer, with an almost totally different repertoire. But this was by the way, though it did make good publicity for the Met.

It is, of course, risky to judge a singer by a single role, but of one thing Miss Farrell's listeners were sure: considered simply as a singer—without regard to such things as repertoire, stagecraft, and experience—she was superior to all three of the Met's supposedly embattled prima donnas. She was more consistently accurate than Miss Milanov; she had a more resonant voice, with a more limpid and pleasing quality, than Miss Callas; and, purely as a vocalist, she far outclassed the unquestionably charming Miss Tebaldi. Moreover, her lung power seemed comparable to that of the illustrious Kirsten Flagstad, and she had an elasticity of voice that Miss Flagstad, at least in her Wagnerian days, did not possess. From these first comparisons, the opera buffs inexorably moved on to the fascinating realm where sopranos, like pugilists, are assigned to various categories. Miss Farrell, it was evident, belonged to the category that the Italians have labeled *soprano drammatica d'agilità*—a fairly rare type, exemplified at that time by Miss Callas, today by Joan Sutherland, and in the remote past by such singers as Lilli Lehmann, Lillian Nordica, Elisabeth Rethberg, and Rosa Ponselle. It was Miss Ponselle to whom Miss Farrell was most often compared by the operatic intelligentsia, and some of them maintained that when it came to refined pianissimos Miss Farrell was the greater artist of the two. The true *soprano drammatica d'agilità*, they all agreed, is in a class by herself. It is she who sings the memorable Normas and other Bellini heroines, the memorable Medeas, Lady Macbeths, and Donna Elviras, and the really memorable Leonoras in Verdi's *Il Trovatore*. With her *agilità*, she is the great virtuoso of the vocal art. While she alone can sing roles like Medea, she can undertake many other roles as well. She can even sing Wagner—a feat that Miss Farrell herself accomplished a few months after her debut in *Medea*, by recording arias from *Tristan und Isolde* and *Götterdämmerung*. A *soprano drammatica d'agilità* appears only a few times in a generation and consequently looms large in the history of opera. The fact that Miss Farrell fell perfectly into this category was shortly confirmed by critics all over the country, and one of them, Alfred Frankenstein, of the San Francisco *Chronicle*, was moved to write, "Miss Farrell has a voice like some unparalleled phenomenon of nature. She is to singers what Niagara is to waterfalls."

The furor that attended Miss Farrell's Medea came as something of a surprise to Miss Farrell herself, and not altogether a

174

pleasant one. While she was understandably proud of her reception at Town Hall and flattered at being considered a possible successor to Lillian Nordica and Rosa Ponselle, she was also a little resentful of the special fuss over what she regarded as just another job of singing. Since this was a craft that she had been pursuing for years, on the radio, at church services, and in concert performances all over the country, she did not much fancy being regarded as a newcomer, however brilliant, who had just been rescued from obscurity. Through a succession of programs presented over the Columbia Broadcasting System—first a sustaining program entitled *Eileen Farrell Sings* and then programs sponsored by such firms as Bayer Aspirin, Coca-Cola, Chrysler Motors, and the Prudential Insurance Company—she had been reaching a much larger audience than any opera house can accommodate, and she was well known on Main Street, if not in the concert halls of the big cities. She had been making quite a lot of money, too, and could certainly be regarded as a success. In the circumstances, she was not inclined to be dazzled by the glittering new world of opera. "Glory be to St. Patrick!" she is reported to have exclaimed to an interviewer after the Town Hall concert. "There's nothing difficult about singing Medea. You just pay attention to the words and do what comes naturally."

Whatever Miss Farrell thought of the furor, it nevertheless propelled her into an entirely new phase of her career. To be sure, she had already made a small name for herself in the field of classical concert music, appearing with the New York Philharmonic in a stage show at the Roxy Theatre in 1950, and participating, from 1953 on, in many of the performances of the local organization known as the Bach Aria Group. None of this, though, had made much of an impression on the operatic audience, and now that it had discovered her, it began applying its exacting standards to her work and demanding that she undertake the great traditional tasks that were commensurate with her abilities. The upshot was the addition of a good deal of operatic work to her concert schedule, several appearances in concert performances of opera (in which the participants, wearing ordinary evening clothes, stand facing the audience and make little effort to act), and even some appearances on real operatic stages in San Francisco and Chicago. About all this, she had certain feelings of ambivalence which have persisted to the present day. When the question arose as to what operatic roles she could sing besides Medea—in which the Opera Society's painstaking conductor, Arnold Gamson, had coached her note for note—the answer was, hardly any. She went on to learn four other roles (Santuzza in *Cavalleria Rusticana*, La Gioconda in the opera of that name, Leonora in *Il Trovatore,* and Ariadne in Richard Strauss' *Ariadne auf Naxos*), but not without some reluctance. Her friends in the musical world admitted that she had only a dim comprehension of the historic grandeur of opera as an art form (it might be remarked that an enlightened comprehension of this is by no means universal among opera singers), and it appeared that she had never regarded the Metropolitan or the famous opera houses of Europe with any particular awe; indeed, in 1945, during the late Edward Johnson's regime as general manager, the Met had offered her a job and she had turned it down in favor of her radio and concert work. She seemed to get as much satisfaction out of singing "Home, Sweet Home" or the "St. Louis Blues" as out of tackling Bellini's "Casta diva," and though she liked being considered an important opera singer, she was annoyed by purists who dismissed her earlier radio appearances as artistically insignificant. She retained an undying loyalty to the musical directors of CBS, who gave her her first chance at celebrity, and she was known occasionally to treat with considerable coolness some of the conductors and directors who had been promoting her as an artistic monument.

These attitudes were variously explained by people who had worked with Miss Farrell. She was not, they pointed out, a self-dramatizing singer like Maria Callas, who existed only for her art and was completely identified with her public personality. Miss

176

Farrell distrusted the operatic world, with all its exotic surroundings, and was extremely anxious to keep her private life aloof from it. According to Allen Sven Oxenburg, the rather Napoleonic impresario of the now defunct American Opera Society, who picked her for the role of Medea after hearing her sing with the Bach Aria Group, she was even a little frightened by her own voice—the noble instrument that, while bringing her fame in musical circles, threatened to launch her onto an unfamiliar sea where she was not yet convinced that she could keep afloat. All the signs, of course, were highly reassuring. But Miss Farrell is an Irish-American with a background completely divorced from opera. Like the late John McCormack, who had something of the same temperament, she was probably doomed to be remembered as a popular entertainer who made a few sensational operatic recordings. That was all right with Miss Farrell. She never *could* figure out what all the fuss about opera meant, and she was making good money on the radio.

However, when Mr. Bing of the Metropolitan read all the publicity about her Medea, he thought of hiring her, and finally he succeeded in signing her up at the Met. She spent only a few years there and thoroughly disliked the place. She dutifully sang the Italian roles that were assigned to her, and the press appreciated her performances. But the big roles that she could have shone in— the brilliant roles nowadays sung by Joan Sutherland, as well as the heavy Wagnerian roles that her voice was especially suited to— were never assigned to her. Opera buffs wrung their hands in frustration, but Mr. Bing was not particularly interested either in the Wagnerian or in the early nineteenth-century bel-canto operas, and Miss Farrell's Metropolitan opera career was wasted on roles that almost any dramatic soprano could sing. What could have become the most glittering star on the operatic horizon was treated like just another singer, and no more furors occurred. When the new Metropolitan Opera House was inaugurated at Lincoln Center, Miss Farrell was not even offered a new contract. It was just like being kicked out. It is easy to blame Mr. Bing. Many vocal experts claim that he never knew what an operatic bombshell he had under his wing. But the fault was also Miss Farrell's, and hers lay in a general lack of enthusiasm for the operatic stage, for Mr. Bing, and for all the fashionable glitter of the opera house.

One factor in all this was unquestionably her marriage to Robert Vincent Reagan, a retired member of the New York City Police Department, who, though he had once been a promising singer of Irish ballads, cared nothing whatever about opera and was certainly ill suited to be a prima donna's husband. He was an outdoorsman, a man of mixed Irish and Italian parentage who liked music if the art is not too strenuously pursued, and a man with an obsession for raising tomato plants. At the time of her first successes, the Reagans lived in a large, neatly kept house on Staten Island, where Miss Farrell took care of two healthy children and was obviously a contented housewife. Her operatic career interfered with this calm domesticity, and the tremor of her great performance as Medea was perhaps less than the tremor it set off in her own mind. If, as she was said to imagine in her gloomier moments, the public loved her only for her voice, there was no doubt that her husband and her children loved her for herself. Basically, both she and her husband considered their family life of far more enduring importance than any career; Miss Farrell's contract with her managers, the Columbia Artists Management, stipulated that she would work no more than two-thirds of each year, and her concert calendar was a curious document on which engagements in New York, San Francisco, Chicago, and countless smaller cities were interspersed with long stretches marked "HOME." "Mama," Mr. Reagan observed to an interviewer at the time, referring to his wife, "was not cut out to be an opera singer. She was meant to have a hundred children." In another interview he said, "I just can't wait to see Mama in a barn milking a cow," and the remark drew nothing but an indulgent smile from Miss Farrell herself.

During her period at the Metropolitan the Reagans moved to an apartment in New York City, but that proved too confining. The move was made not only because of the Met, but also because their son, Robert Reagan, Jr., won a scholarship at Fordham University. The son was very enthusiastic about ROTC and wanted to spend his final year at the University of New Hampshire. Miss Farrell never got to milk a cow, nor did she have a hundred children (she had two; a daughter named Kathleen followed their son), but Mr. Reagan did get to raise tomato plants. Both offspring are now adults, Robert, Jr., having served as an Air Force officer. For the past ten years the Reagans have spent their summers at a camp at Moosehead Lake in Maine, where they have five boats. "We really rough it," Miss Farrell says. "I also play golf. It's the greatest thing I've ever discovered." A few years ago the family moved to the University of Indiana, which has the largest music school in the world, an opera house, and about thirty thousand students, and Miss Farrell, with her children grown, has taken up teaching voice there, living in a large house with a garden where her husband can grow his tomato plants.

The Reagans keep pretty much to themselves, attending an occasional cocktail party and hating it thoroughly. They drink and smoke in moderation, and Mr. Reagan claims that his wife's only vice is an uncontrollable addiction to supermarkets, which she sometimes visits twice a day. During her days with the Metropolitan, Miss Farrell's professional colleagues reported occasional fits of smoldering resentment in which she expressed herself in a fine vocabulary of Irish expletives. But at home she is a sunny-tempered, loud-laughing, and obviously contented woman, untroubled by anything in the way of driving ambition and eager to be accepted for what she is offstage—a diligent housewife, grateful for such homely pleasures as her situation affords. The Reagans' attitude toward home and family at one time brought them into repeated conflict with the romantic esthetes of the musical world. Once Mr. Oxenburg, finding himself up against the couple's adamant domesticity, lost his temper and exclaimed indignantly to Mr. Reagan, "For heaven's sake, there are sixty million mamas in

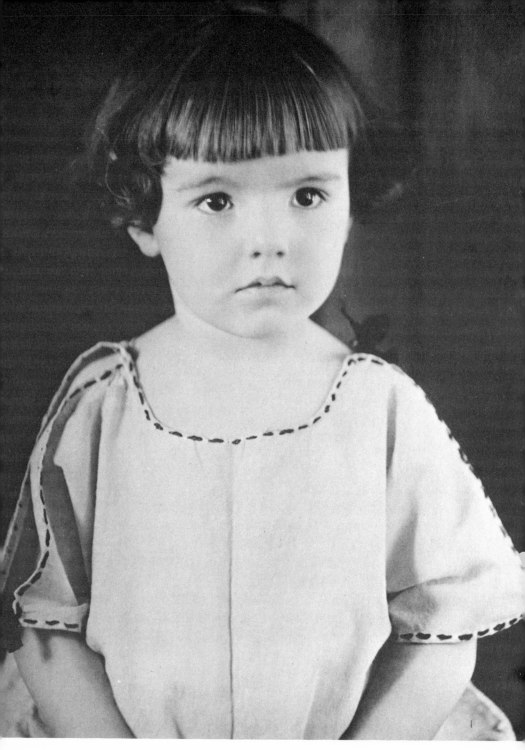

Miss Farrell as a child.

Miss Farrell's family. *Left to right:* Her husband, Robert Vincent Reagan, Kathleen, Robert, Jr., and Miss Farrell.

Photograph by Louis Mélançon

Miss Farrell as Maddalena in Umberto Giordano's *Andrea Chénier*.

Photograph by Louis Mélançon

As La Gioconda in *La Gioconda* by Ponchielli.

America, but there is only one Eileen Farrell." And, more recently, several New York impresarios have been rebuffed by Mr. Reagan in their attempts to get her for New York appearances. The family has thus far remained unmoved by such assaults on the serenity of its private life. And though, for a long time after her debut with the American Opera Society, she continued to sing with them (for more than their usual fee), she carried on a long feud with Mr. Oxenburg. "I can communicate with him only by swearing at him," she remarked at one point. And her communications with Mr. Bing of the Metropolitan were no more cordial.

The other resentments that ruffle Miss Farrell's placidity usually arise when she thinks she is being used unfairly or when other people behave in a manner she considers dishonest. For a long time, she had no press agent, believing firmly that she should stand or fall on her own merits, and when she was at the Chicago Opera back in the sixties and was approached by the head of the claque asking whether she would like to purchase some applause, she simply swore and showed him the door. As it turned out, her unbought applause was thunderous, and that gave her immense satisfaction. On another occasion the late Dorothy Kilgallen heard and printed a touching but inaccurate story that had her making repeated trips to Brooklyn to teach a crippled boy how to sing. Any other diva would have let it pass. But Miss Farrell immediately got Miss Kilgallen on the phone, told her that there wasn't a word of truth in the story, and adjured her, in strong language, never to mention her name again.

Miss Farrell occasionally still emerges from her domesticity to sing with some symphony orchestra or to give a series of recitals in small towns that other stars would not deign to visit. She also sings in New York nearly every year, either in a recital or with the New York Philharmonic under Leonard Bernstein or with some visiting orchestra. Some of these forays involve what might be called small tours on which she has to sleep in hotels. Generally she keeps to her hotel room, avoiding all the fuss of after-concert parties, and spends her time reading detective stories. "Maybe I'm lowbrow," she said a while ago, "but I like mysteries. The trouble with high-class novels is that they don't have good plots." In opera, too, she likes good plots and good characters. "You take Leonora in *Trovatore*," she went on. "What does she do? She just stands around and sings. She's a real nothin'. Now, La Gioconda and Santuzza, they're real women. They give you something to get your teeth into. And Medea—well, she's a horror, of course, but she's a real woman, too. Imagine murdering your children to spite an unfaithful husband!" Miss Farrell may be a conventional housewife, and she may have very little idea of the cultural and historical ramifications of opera, but, given the role of a woman she can understand, she can play it to the hilt. Mr. Oxenburg recalls lecturing Miss Farrell on the historical significance of Cherubini's *Medea,* the lecture producing nothing much but a series of "uh-huhs." But when the conductor, Arnold Gamson, in the course of training her in the role and explaining its psychology, said, "Here you practically lose your mind—you are an absolute bitch," Miss Farrell methodically wrote BITCH in large letters above the notes at that point in the score, and from that moment on she was the answer to an impresario's prayer.

In general, as befits a housewife with a distaste for the esoteric and highfalutin, Miss Farrell has a matter-of-fact approach to the arcana of opera. Like many Irish-Americans, and, indeed, many north Europeans, she considers song a vehicle for poetic and dramatic ideas, and looks down on the conception of it—popular in Italy—as a vehicle for athletic display. When, for example, she is asked where she acquired the remarkable classical style that characterizes her performances, she is somewhat at a loss for an explanation, usually saying simply, "I just pay attention to the words and try to express what they say." While this throws a good deal of light on her attitude toward singing, it fails to indicate where the refined classical style actually did come from, and the problem continues to preoccupy connoisseurs, who regard such a style with considerable awe and usually think of it as the product of the most intensive study. The answer, perhaps, is to be found partly in Miss Farrell's innate feeling for music, partly in her association long ago for many years with the Bach Aria Group, a very serious troupe with which she tackled the most exacting of all vocal tasks—those posed by the cantatas of Johann Sebastian Bach. But some of it may also have come from her early family environment and training. For Miss Farrell is the daughter of two professional singers and has been singing herself since childhood.

Eileen Farrell's father, the late Michael Farrell, was a Newfoundlander whose grandparents came from Ireland, and, as a boy soprano and an adult baritone, he was involved in church singing and show business for most of his life. Her mother, the former Catherine Kennedy, who was a teacher of singing in Woonsocket, Rhode Island, was inclined to deprecate the Irishness of the family, pointing out that *her* people came over much earlier than her husband's and that her grandfather was a Union soldier in the Civil War. In any case, Michael Farrell settled in Woonsocket early in this century and met Miss Kennedy while both were singing in the Catholic church choir. They were married in 1909 and soon set themselves up as a team known as the Singing O'Farrells, touring widely in New England as both a church and a vaudeville attraction and singing everything from Latin hymns to Irish sentimental ballads. By the time Eileen was born, in 1920, the Farrells had settled in Willimantic, Connecticut, and moved shortly thereafter to Storrs, where Farrell organized the male glee club of the University of Connecticut and supervised undergraduate drama performances, while his wife organized the female glee club and gave singing lessons. The elder Farrell, as his daughter remembers him, was a perfectionist who spent hours every day listening to her first efforts at singing and criticizing them unsparingly.

From the first, the Farrells realized that Eileen had a voice of unusual caliber, and when the girl graduated from high school in 1939, her mother decided that it was time to send her to New York for systematic training. The contralto Merle Alcock, who had sung at the Metropolitan and was then giving lessons, was an acquaintance of Mrs. Farrell's, and it was arranged that she would take Eileen under her wing. Mrs. Alcock considered the young singer very promising indeed, and in addition to charging her usual fee, she stipulated that she should receive a cut of ten percent on whatever Eileen earned in her future as a singer. The relationship between teacher and pupil did not turn out to be an entirely satisfactory one. Eileen took a little room in the Evangeline, a residence for young women on West Thirteenth Street, but she was not happy either with New York or with Mrs. Alcock, and several times she wrote her mother that she couldn't stand her life there and wanted to return home. Mrs. Farrell, however, insisted that she persevere. One of the main troubles was that Mrs. Alcock, a tempestuous and demanding woman, had Eileen doing more than just musical chores. Eileen recalls that she sewed the diva's clothes, did her cooking, ran her errands, and took care of her invalid sister. "I must say that Mrs. Alcock didn't do my voice any harm," Miss Farrell remarks, paying her old teacher what everybody who has investigated the queer, superstitious, mountebank-ridden world inhabited by vocal teachers in New York must regard as a positive tribute. "But she didn't help my nerves any."

While studying with Mrs. Alcock, Eileen made a few efforts in the direction of a public career. Early in 1940, she submitted herself as a candidate for the *Major Bowes Amateur Hour;* she got as far as rehearsals and then was eliminated by the major, who decided she wasn't good enough. A few weeks later she got an audition with the Columbia Broadcasting System, where two members of the system's casting department—James Fassett and Lucile Singleton—gave her a job singing in choruses and ensembles and doing other routine assignments. Her first week's pay was sixty-nine dollars and thirty cents, and Mrs. Alcock promptly got her six ninety-three. Miss Farrell's first real claim to public attention came on October 16, 1941, when, in a historical documentary on *The March of Time,* she sang three measures of "Home Sweet Home," impersonating the voice of Rosa Ponselle. The job paid good money for the three measures involved, and a few months later CBS put her on a series of radio programs aimed at its Southern affiliates, in which she sang mostly Stephen Foster, and then gave her star billing with *Eileen Farrell Sings,* a weekly half hour devoted to art songs, lieder, and arias. To Miss Farrell this was the top of the heap. Opera? What was opera? A lot of stuffed shirts listening to singers with foreign names.

One of the more ardent fans of *Eileen Farrell Sings* was Robert Reagan, a member of the Police Department Glee Club, an amateur Irish-type tenor of some pretensions, and a fervent lover of fine song. It happened that soon after the program got under way, Mr. Reagan, who was then a plainclothesman attached to the forgery squad, was working on a case of blackmail designed to victimize Herman Patrick Tappé, of the House of Tappé, a couturier's establishment on West Fifty-seventh Street, and it also happened at the time that Mr. Tappé was making some clothes for Miss Farrell. Mr. Reagan and Mr. Tappé became rather chummy, and one day in August, 1942, after Mr. Reagan had expressed his admiration for Miss Farrell's voice, the couturier suggested that he and Reagan have lunch together, adding casually that they would be joined by somebody he would probably like to meet. "Now, to be honest," Mr. Reagan says "I had never particularly wanted to meet anybody, unless it was a hunter or a fisherman, but I went along." They went to the Gripsholm Restaurant, and the policeman was introduced to his favorite singer. The result was crucial in the lives of both Mr. Reagan and Miss Farrell. They went steady for several years and were married on April 4, 1946.

The marriage involved a good many personal adjustments, and in the beginning Mr. Reagan, who was presently transferred to Staten Island, where they took up residence, found doubling as a policeman and the husband of a noted singer something of a strain. "For a while," he remembers, "I considered calling myself Mr.

Farrell, but I decided I couldn't take that." On one matter, Mr. Reagan put his foot down even before the wedding, and that was the status of Miss Farrell vis-à-vis Mrs. Alcock. Once he had looked the relationship over, he decided it should be broken off. "The wife never would have been able to do it on her own," he explained. "She's too loyal to anybody who has ever done anything for her." But under his prodding she made the break, in 1944, terminating the ten percent arrangement and looking elsewhere for coaching and vocal training.

Professional singers, like athletes, require the ministrations of expert trainers—in the singer's case, voice-placement specialists, repertoire coaches, language teachers, and conductors or assistant conductors who are interested in preparing a singer for one role or another—right up to the end of their careers. In New York, many of these trainers inhabit studios located near Lincoln Center, in Carnegie Hall and the buildings surrounding it, and in the old Ansonia Hotel, at Broadway and Seventy-third Street—an edifice whose thick masonry walls seem specially designed to minimize the clamor of vocal instruction and practice. The trainers live in a world of their own—a world in which a pianissimo high C or a correctly articulated vowel is regarded as one of the greatest achievements in life. A large number of them, unfortunately, are quacks, who can ruin the delicate mechanism of the singing voice in no time, but some of them are cultivated pedagogues, with a profound knowledge not only of the traditions of singing, but also of such anatomical matters as are involved in the fruitful use, for vocal purposes, of the lungs, larynx, and the oral and nasal channels. The real expert in this field is at once an experienced musician, a sort of vocal pathologist, and an artist in the building and maintaining of fine voices. The services of the better trainers are much in demand, and word of their virtues passes from singer to singer. Though the public seldom hears of them, they are regarded with deep respect within the profession, and they are undoubtedly responsible, indirectly, for many of the golden tones and feats of style that are projected over the footlights in places like the Metropolitan.

Shortly after breaking with Mrs. Alcock, Miss Farrell had the good fortune to be introduced by a friend to one of these people—a financially independent widow named Eleanor McLellan, who inhabited a cluttered, old-fashioned studio in the Ansonia Hotel. Mrs. McLellan, herself formerly a singer, as well as a harpist, violinist, and pianist, had devoted most of a long lifetime to the problems of this particular craft, teaching and advising singers since the time of Lillian Nordica, who was a distant relative of hers. When she met Miss Farrell, she proposed that the singer visit her studio. Miss Farrell did. A bond grew up between the two women, based—on Miss Farrell's part at least—on incalculable gratitude. At the outset, Mrs. McLellan brushed aside any question of payment for her services, and proposed to coach her new pupil gratis. "The moment I heard her," she remarked to an interviewer, "I knew that this was singing in the grand old-time manner. She had power galore. Her only fault was that she couldn't sing pianissimo. It was a fault that Rosa Ponselle had, too, and we started correcting it." The exact process of correction remains one of those mysteries known only to voice teachers, but in any case it meant hard work for Miss Farrell, who went regularly to Mrs. McLellan's studio, and set to work mastering Bach arias by first learning the words, then speaking them in rhythm with the music, and finally singing them. Mrs. McLellan, whom Miss Farrell soon began referring to as "Mama," noted and carefully checked every response of the Farrell voice, laying special emphasis on the production and enunciation of vowels. The strategy certainly worked, for Miss Farrell soon became a much more sensitive and controlled singer than she had been, and in addition, the range of her voice was considerably enlarged.

In 1947, when radio began to be overwhelmed by television, Miss Farrell, who could never envision herself as a successful television personality ("I'm not much of an actress," she explained), began seriously considering a career as a concert artist, and in the fall of that year she signed up with a concert manager, the late Horace Parmelee, who started her off on a lively schedule of out-of-town engagements. Her reasons for the switch seem to have been economic rather than purely artistic, and even today she regards singing more as a method of making a living than a glamorous artistic enterprise. From the start, she had plenty of work in the United States and Canada, and between recitals she made recordings, sang with symphony orchestras, and had her voice dubbed in on sound tracks for the movies. The pay was good, and for a long time she saw no reason for competing with internationally famous prima donnas.

Fame and acknowledged artistry are insidious things, though, and after her historic *Medea* performance, Miss Farrell began to think, however hesitantly, of singing in terms of prestige, as well as money. She began curbing her healthy appetite for the sake of her figure and succeeded in losing some weight. On the visual side, her acting began to take on some animation, and she began paying more attention to matters of costume—always of extreme importance to a big woman who wants to sing opera. By the time she got to the Metropolitan (she had already sung to great acclaim at the San Francisco and Chicago operas), her appearance onstage had become plump rather than ponderous. The dieting did not seem to affect her voice, though some listeners detected, or thought they detected, evidences of strain from time to time. Medea, her most famous role at the time, is, even in concert form, one of the most strenuous workouts a soprano can undergo, and she sang it on tour from one end of the country to another with the patient muscular energy of a truck horse. On the subject of weight, she can be either good-natured or slightly touchy, depending on the attitude of the person she is talking to. Long ago a noted conductor who is not remarkable for his height asked her teasingly, "Miss Farrell, how much do you weigh?" "Two hundred and twenty pounds," she said, and added, "How tall are you?"

As for Europe, Miss Farrell never had any particular ambitions to sing there. She did make a trip to Berlin to sing in a concert under the auspices of the American National Theatre and Academy, a long time ago. But this was an affair of diplomatic, rather than strictly musical, importance and therefore, unfortunately, was not attended either by that city's more exacting critics or by much of its equally exacting musical audience. Miss Farrell stayed in Berlin for a couple of days and then went to London to make some recordings for Angel Records. During this trip, she telephoned her husband every day, and within two weeks she was back on Staten Island, where she immediately proceeded to bake a cake. She made a trip to Europe in 1959, singing recitals in London and at Gian Carlo Menotti's festival at Spoleto, and she has made a trip to Puerto Rico to sing at the Casals Festival there. Everywhere she has gone she has remained just long enough to accomplish her mission. As for Mr. Reagan, he accepted his wife's absences philosophically. He didn't go with her to Europe. As he once remarked, "What's the use of traveling to foreign parts when there's so much beautiful nature to see right here in America?"

And with this point Miss Farrell concurred. "My greatest ambition is to retire from all this touring and singing," she once told a reporter. "What I really like to do is stay home with my family." And that is about what she has been doing recently, apart from her duties as a teacher at the University of Indiana. Still, from time to time, Miss Farrell does emerge from her quiet existence to sing with some symphony orchestra or to give a recital. She has, among other things, recently made a recording of Donizetti's opera *Maria Stuarda* with Beverly Sills. She also made one as Maria in Berg's *Wozzeck* long ago under the baton of Dimitri Mitropoulos for Columbia Records. Over the door of her studio at the University of Indiana there is a sign reading "Help Stamp Out Opera." Humor? Partly. Most singers love their work. But Miss Farrell has always had ambivalent feelings toward it. For her, it has always been primarily a job and not always a congenial one.